"Tom Donnan's book, *Healing* [illegible] the prophetic journey as an alarm cl[illegible] others, Tom also has experienced physically dying and coming back to life. His experiential message by his new lease on life to stay here and obey God to fulfill His calling from Jesus Christ, heightens the ever-increasing necessity to pray and turn our nation back to the heart of our Father God! Tom includes a delightful family setting, the pursuit of the truth in ministry including honoring the prophetic gifts of God to share with us this "now word" of reconnecting our family values to join Heaven's values with the Kingdom family in earth as it is in heaven.

"Be encouraged that Tom also shares the importance of hearing God, taking Him at His Word, and then obeying His call. Be refreshed as I was to take Tom's adventurous life journey into your heart with reassurance that you too can fulfill the destiny as God has designed to further God's Kingdom now! This a message to bring us all to our knees and our walk with God to take our nation back for God! We will do this; it is just how we live with the results that determine if we obey! Thank you Tom Donnan for your heart to cause us all in the land of the free and the home of the brave to again be the 'One Nation Under God' because we as believer's will indeed, inherit the land as American's in this hour." —*John Mark Pool, Prophetic Evangelist, Author, Co-founder of Word to the World Ministries, www.w2wmin.org*

"Several years ago, I received an e-mail from a total stranger, Tom Donnan, inquiring about revival in Texas. Tom was so inquisitive about the revival fires burning, along with events in and around an outpouring of His Presence in Texas. Tom has been given keen insight to what God is doing and the direction He is going and wanted to pull from me as much information as he could. Tom's interest and the questions he asked, equaled my passion in sharing what God is doing in the Lone Star State.

"Tom is a man that God is raising up in the Body that operates with very keen insight into the spiritual dimension. God frequently visits Tom with dreams and open visions. My years of pastoral experience have taught me that it is very necessary to carefully scrutinize the ministry of such. I have found Tom to be very accurate into spiritual matters and he is very scripture based.

"In my own life and ministry, God gives Tom information only to find that it involves a person I am about to minister to or to a congregation as I prepare to minister. On one of my international ministry trips recently, God showed Tom the physical location I was going to minister, as well as the spiritual climate, even details of strangers that I was about to be ministering to. Tom comes alongside me in a supportive role and makes the thing I am called to do, much more effective.

"You will always find him in the shadows of the church service, watching, praying, and hearing from God. Often, when I travel and minister, I find men with the same gift, but they become somewhat of a stumbling block to me as they attempt to help. He has probably one of the most generous hearts of any man that I have ever met. He is willing to stand in the wings, to serve the Body in the venue in which he is called.

"I am excited about this project that Tom has completed. I know this book is the result of many hours of burning the midnight oil. He has spent so much time searching the scriptures as well as the heart of the Father to obtain his information. Tom often travels with me and brings his teaching ministry to a congregation and prepares them to receive from the ministry that God has placed before me." —*Pastor Phillip Corbett, First Assembly of God, Corrigan, Texas, Founder of Second Wind Ministries*

"Tom Donnan's insight into dreams and visions has been a God-send to me and my family. Before meeting Tom, my wife and I truly never had known the depths of our dreams and how they affected our lives. If it were not for Tom's insights into this spiritual realm, I would not know how to interpret the morning I woke up still smelling the burning embers of smoke all over my body after one of my dreams. Tom is truly a man after God's own heart and a cherished Christian brother and friend that I know I can go to when a dream arrives that I cannot grasp or understand." —*Ben Dupré*

"After reading this amazing book, I can fully understand and appreciate Tom's journey. His hard work and dedication have taken him to extreme levels of knowing and understanding God. This growth enabled him to take on new adventures and challenges in accepting his godly appointment. I observed the progression of an honest, hard-working man intensify for greater purposes other than for being just a loving, family provider. He has yielded to God and developed into a blessing for many. I pray that the message in his dreams will stimulate the hearts of the masses and a crucial transformation will flood our country. Wake up America!" —*Marlene Kluch*

Healing the Nation

Tom Donnan

Mobile, Alabama

Healing the Nation
by Tom Donnan
Copyright ©2013 Tom Donnan

Unless otherwise identified, Scripture is taken from *THE HOLY BIBLE: New International Version* ©1978 by the New York International Bible Society, used by permission of Zondervan Bible Publishers. Scripture marked NLT are taken from the Holy Bible, New Living Translation, copyright ©1996. Used by permission of Tyndale House Publishers, Inc., Wheaton IL 60189. Scripture marked NKJ are taken from the New King James Version. Copyright © 1982 by Thomas Nelson, Inc.

Cover design by C.J. McDaniel

ISBN 978-1-58169-473-4
For Worldwide Distribution
Printed in the U.S.A.
Gazelle Press
P.O. Box 191540 • Mobile, AL 36619
800-367-8203

"For I know the plans I have for you," declares the LORD, "plans to prosper you and not to harm you, plans to give you hope and a future" (Jeremiah 29:11-12).

And we know that in all things God works for the good of those who love him, who have been called according to his purpose (Romans 8:28).

The thief comes only to steal and kill and destroy; I have come that they may have life, and hive it to the full (John 10:10).

To God is all the glory for His work in and through my life.
How could I have known that He would bring me
to a place of ministering to pastors and people?
On February 6, 2006, I had my second heart attack
and this time I died.
While out of my body, I heard Him speak to me.
He said "It is only while you are on Earth
that you can work for Jesus!"
I am grateful for my extra time
to work for the Lord.

Contents

Acknowledgments

I love new adventures, do you? It has been because of my wife Mary's support that this book as come to fruition. I have spent many hours in the pursuit of sharing God's vision with others. Mary has been there every step of the way. Our grown children have been very positive in my endeavor, and it has been energizing. Thanks to all of those who have helped and strategized with me, especially Christine and my good friend Marlene.

To all the following pastors who have given me the okay to use their names and churches in telling my story, I sincerely thank you.

- Pastor Phillip Corbett
- Pastor Glynn
- Pastor Jimmie
- Pastor Lynn
- Pastor Shannon
- Pastor Becky
- Pastor John Mark Pool
- Pastor Mark
- Pastor Joshua

Also, I would like to thank my extended family and friends who have been my support along the way.

Introduction

I call myself an experiential Christian because I have been in the process of making meaning out of my direct experiences. For two decades, I searched to understand my walk with Jesus.

After Hurricane Katrina, I heard about a pastor, who had prophesied that New Orleans was going to be under water, six months before the hurricane. Because of this prophecy, I wanted to meet the one who gave it—Pastor John Mark Pool.

The closest his schedule brought him to my home in the Chicago area was Cleveland, Ohio. The event was a three-day teaching on connecting with the prophetic. This was something that I was experiencing, but I just couldn't put the pieces together and needed some help. I signed up for the meetings, took the time off from work, and reserved my hotel room. Only fifteen people had signed up—there were not many people seeking to understand the spiritual gift from God. With these odds, I was looking forward to having a chance at some one-on-one time with Pastor John Mark.

This meeting was a turning point for me—it brought me some understanding of my spiritual life and future. I am sharing the stories and accounts of my personal experiences to contribute to the changing of America and transforming the church.

I have lived most of my Christian life in a hidden place of God. I thought there were more people who were living an experiential life, as I have been. In this last year, I have come to understand why my life in Jesus Christ is different. I experience things of His spiritual Kingdom often. No wonder people had a hard time with me—even my wife had difficulties in grasping my spiritual life at times.

Why is my life different? God was getting me ready to help in the turbulent times ahead. He has been preparing a remnant to be released, and the time is here and now! The heart and soul of this book is centered on a life-changing vision that I received on January 20, 2006. In addition to this vision, there are warnings of serious change coming to America in which we could lose our freedom as Americans.

• I pray you can see that there is more in our Christian walk than we are currently experiencing.

• I pray that you will benefit by grasping the vision for yourself and your families.

• I pray that you will take part in the prayers for our country.

• I pray that God will bring you to a new spiritual position in life.

• I pray that your personal journey into repentance will have a major impact on a course correction for America.

America is headed toward destruction of our current way of life. We have been accustomed to a life of freedom that we have loved with all our hearts and would like to pass on to future generations. Everyone is needed to change the direction in which America is headed. You and your family can make that important difference now!

Chapter 1

Saying Yes to God

The Art of Friendship[1] is a book that challenged me to risk reaching out to others in friendship. I needed it! I was lonely and needed friendship beyond my wife and family. Through it I learned one principle that to this day, I still practice: When you are extended invitations to events, you need to accept them more than you reject them. My automatic response to invitations had been usually: "No thanks!" I decided to rewrite that internal program, which is easier said than done. I began to quickly say yes before I could talk myself out of an invitation. When I was younger, relationships and friendships hadn't worked out very well for me and so I had conditioned myself to respond in a protection mode.

When I came to the place where it was time to lower the walls I had built around myself and leave my manmade island, I accepted the challenge with faith that God was in it.

Meeting throngs of people is now an everyday thing for me. During my scheduled work for the month, I may visit more than seventy buildings in my territory. My largest account, a medical facility with a trauma hospital, sits on a piece of property that is one block wide by two blocks long. Thousands of people work there. I had to learn, in the cafeteria, to squeeze between elbows and push through with apologies in order to get to the checkout line.

I am a growing Christian—growing 24/7. My work environment includes a portion of my experience with growth, as well where I live out my faith in Jesus Christ. I try to make it known to the people with whom I am in contact that I am a Christian. I establish my position of faith and I am open about it. I have forty units to service and maintain at that hospital. Part of servicing these units—a combination of elevators, dumbwaiters, and cart lifts—is to order replacement parts. When my order comes in, it arrives at the loading dock and enters the Shipping and Receiving Department. There are ten people laboring to keep up with the flow of incoming deliveries for a medical facility of this size. In this organized chaos, I met Ken.

The guys have a special place assigned for my stuff, and the first desk in the doorway to the department is Ken's. He openly lives out his faith. He brings God and Jesus into his conversation with natural ease. I was impressed with how easily he accomplishes the transition from worldly opinions to biblical principles. Ken and I became fast friends. After being challenged by the book *The Art of Friendship*, I was ready. I leaped without caution and accepted when he gave me an invitation to his church's Christmas presentation.

Singles Group

My wife and I were already on staff at a different church as directors of the singles group, which is where we met. It was a great time until a virus broke out and half of the group caught the bug—marriage—and the numbers dwindled for a time! The upside was obvious: finding a partner for life. But the downside was that married people were no longer allowed to participate in the singles group. We were drafted by the church to continue in the singles group by leading it.

After our marriage, our schedules were full. Both of us were working full-time jobs and coordinating the singles meetings every Monday night. It was our first experience leading and directing an organized group. It was a lot of work that included lining up speakers and organizing special events. We also gathered the material for the weekly meetings, planned group discussions and activities, and made sure there was time for fellowship (mingling). It took awhile for us to learn about all the details and the scheduling needed so that the meetings would flow without a hitch. We were seeing firsthand what happens behind the scenes of an organized event. It gave me an appreciation for Ken's invitation, knowing how much rehearsal time the church members were volunteering in preparation for their Christmas outreach event.

Outreach

Ken's church sent out a mass mailing to the surrounding community announcing the Christmas presentation. Ten thousand postcards were distributed with a personal invitation to come and join the church in their celebration of the birth of Jesus. (Trivia fact: In churches that use mass mailings, their expected response from the community took me by surprise. I was shocked to hear that for every one thousand postcards sent out, ten people will respond. One percent!) In addition to the post-cards, more effective is the word-of-mouth invitation, such as I received from Ken. Here the response is much higher. Both the postcards and personal invitations were going to bring in new people, and that was the major point of focus.

Anticipation of Christmas is a wonderful feeling. My wife and I try to plan events throughout the month of December with family and friends. It extends the joy the season. Attending the presentation that night fit right into the scheme of things. It was the Saturday before Christmas. It was already dark when we arrived. I made the turn off the main street, drove one-quarter block to the driveway and looked for the best parking spot available in the lot. I think we were both surprised with the country feel of the church. The community had been built up around this time-stamped location.

With every new thing in life, we were a bit nervous, not knowing exactly what to expect. But being there was the beginning of an im-proved friendship with Ken that had grown over the years.

Taking the Risk

The entrance to the church started with a concrete stairway at the top of which was a landing with a black wrought-iron railing around it. The front door was a double-hung, center-opening, solid wood door with a square window set on the diamond. No sooner had we climbed the stairs, when the front door swung open by an extending arm of the friendly church greeter. No turning back now! Handshakes and small talk softened the first nervous impression. We were handed off to the usher, who greeted us with a warm smile and said, "Follow me." We walked a short distance through the breezeway and into the back of the sanctuary.

To my relief, we were seated near the back of the church. (I would improve at dealing with this "front row phobia" later on in life.) If the church was full, there would be about four hundred people in attendance. That night, I guessed that there were some two hundred and fifty people taking part in the service.

I was paying attention to the building's layout. This portion of the church had a rectangular section. The sanctuary and cry room were separated by a partial wall that had wooden panels on the bottom and large glass windows on the top. Whoever was in the cry room area could see through into the sanctuary and still be part of the service. It seemed they were a thoughtful church, ready to meet the needs of young families.

We were led to the south side of the church, through doors and up the aisle.

Unexpected Surprise

One thing I have learned in life is that "all things are possible with God." I was there at the invitation of Ken. Yet God had me there to show me a totally different picture—a church in bondage! We pray, seek, and knock at His door so that we may be gifted by the Holy Spirit to be a vessel used of Jesus to bless the Kingdom of God. My gift, as I am still learning each and every day, is to see into the spiritual realm. I then convey what is happening there and how it is affecting a person, church, place, or region. Being spiritually sensitive helps me to be aware of God's guidance around me. That night, I was totally unprepared for a peek behind the veil and into the spiritual realm of what was happening to the pastor and the people he was there to impact. I was about to embark on a new journey.

The Performance

As my father would describe some services, it was a "Sunday-go-to-meetin'" kind of service. We enjoyed the traditional Christmas hymns and uplifting songs of praise and worship. There was a five-member worship team. Ken played the guitar and led us to lift our hearts toward Jesus in gratitude and thanksgiving. It brought back one of those wonderful holiday remembrances from my childhood when as a family we all sang Christmas carols and hymns. The next feature of the evening was music played by the pastor's daughter who was home from college. She was a music major, and we were blessed to hear her beautiful voice and unbelievable talent at the piano. I thought I had gone to a concert hall. That evening was filled with so much musical talent that it moved my heart and soul. Without our noticing, the pastor slipped away from his seat and moved over to the podium. He began to speak as the piano softly played. Where did the time go? We were now moving into the message stage of the program.

Spiritual Life

I estimate that I have heard over two thousand Sunday sermons in my lifetime, maybe more. I remember the day, even the hour, when I passed from death to life. It was May 7, 1983, at 6:30 p.m. when I invited Jesus into my life and heart. Before being born again, I spent the better part of twenty-five years attending church and hadn't come face-to-face with the holy and true God by the Holy Spirit. It is an amazing story but not part of this day. This day God was using the gifts He has built in me to see a problem that was a hindrance to the labors and energy of this pastor. He was investing his heart and soul into this church and the community by spreading the saving knowledge of Jesus Christ. He was laboring to reveal the light of the Gospel and let it shine before his congregation. I was amazed! As I listened to this pastor, truly, a river of living water flowed from him. He was spiritually speaking from the podium toward the people. Here was a man who had gone through trials, storms, and struggles. He was a God-ordained minister walking in the anointing to preach the Gospel.

I was totally engaged in every word that he was speaking. I could almost feel my thirst for knowing God being satisfied while he spoke. I sat in my pew, leaning forward as if to more quickly receive the word he was sharing by making it a shorter distance between me and the podium for the pastor's spiritual life to reach my soul. I was shocked and in awe. These words of life were so refreshing. Suddenly quickened by the Holy Spirit, I began to look around. I looked for signs to see if the people around me were being impacted. I wanted to see the effects this gift of God was having on them. Nothing! I could see little to no impact reaching the hearts and souls of the people! What was happening? What was wrong?

Puzzled and Questioning

There are some speakers whom I can listen to for hours. This pastor's message ended way too soon. He closed the evening with a benediction, and then Ken came down the aisle toward us from the front row where he had been sitting with his wife. They invited us downstairs for a time of food and fellowship. Not knowing exactly where to go, we followed him out the main doorway. Exiting the sanctuary, we were greeted by the pastor, who was waiting to shake hands and speak a warm word to everyone. I was so excited to meet him and I said, "Pastor, you are an anointed preacher, to preach the Gospel." This is something any pastor would like to hear. In a situation like this, there was no time for any extended conversation, so I left it at that. It did bring a broad smile to his face. He said, "Thanks," and we made our way to the food.

Newcomer's Nervousness

The final part of the Christmas program—the meet-and-greet! We made our way over to the treat tables, and I picked out cookies, a piece of cake, and several other items. The deacons and elders of the church were walking among the crowd. They were stepping forward to introduce themselves and engage everyone. There were a number of new people, including ourselves. Ken gladly introduced us around. I was really happy we had accepted his invitation. It enriched my life and brought me to a new adventure with God.

If you are like me, a new spiritual adventure means spending a lot of time praying and asking the Lord what I could learn from my new experience. It was several days later when I had a chance to talk with Ken about the Christmas service. He was anxious to hear what I had to say about his church and the experience. I think I surprised him with my observations. What can I say, I was shocked. God's quickening and revelations don't happen to me every day. I believe what I saw and experienced helped Ken to connect a dream he had concerning his church. So when I got to the part of what little impact the preaching seemed to have on the people, Ken surprised me. He shared with me the details of a powerful dream he had concerning his church. Now, let me interject here and share my understanding of dreams and visions. I have come to know there are times and people to whom God does speak in dreams and visions to convey information for a purpose concerning the Kingdom of God. Ken is a man who seeks after God's heart. He had a dream that gave him an understanding of what was happening in his church, and it was an answer to his prayers.

Concisely put, Ken shared that the Lord had shown him a demonic spirit of tradition that ran around the sanctuary pews, separating the pastor from the people. The pastor's anointed words of God hit an invisible spiritual wall and fell short of the hearts they were intended to reach. Now you may ask, "How could that be? Isn't a church a sacred place of God?" Churches are buildings, like any other building. However, using spiritual principles of anointing and prayer, they can be set apart and made holy so that the presence of God abides in them.

It is when sin enters that a change happens, and spiritual ownership changes hands from godly to evil. Now the sins we are talking about vary in intensity and violation. For example, corporate sins of the church leadership open a door to sin and its downward effects. These are called grounds, and evil enters the place until the grounds are forgiven and the effects are removed. So the spiritual atmosphere of a church can be stymied by sin. When a new pastor arrives on the scene, he may be blinded to what is happening behind the spiritual veil. Now, I totally agreed with what Ken was shown. So let's move on to the next step. What part did God intend for me to play now that I had seen this?

Chapter 2

Plan of Action

Prophecy and gifting in the prophetic are really tough for me to deal with. That is why I was so blessed to have a pastor to talk to. He heard about all the spiritual things I was experiencing.

I don't particularly like to recall the early days when I was trying to understand the messages God shared with me. I was so excited to be a part of what God was doing that I often only got some of the message right. For years, I walked in prophetic immaturity. I was stumbling through the learning process. Sometimes I even made a mess of things. What I see in the spiritual realm, through God's symbolism, is a constant struggle for me. I try to put my experience into words to be able to share the message with others. What degree of difficulty is it? It all happens in the translation from human reasoning to grasping spiritual interactions with God. He states in scripture:

> *"For my thoughts are not your thoughts, neither are your ways my ways," declares the Lord* (Isaiah 55:8).

Knowing the Scriptures is vitally important to gain an understanding of His ways! I have interactions with the Lord that I know are important. When He has shown me information, I take that responsibility very seriously. And so I once again sought out the advice of my pastor, relaying to him the whole story of Ken's church. I asked him, "What should I do?" He said, "Wait!" The advice became clear to me in the days following the meeting with my pastor.

When God shows me something, it might be days, weeks, months, or even years in advance. I was to see the leadings of the Father and I was to wait until the timing was right to step forward. It was His plan, not mine. This time it took from December of that year until late October of the next year before I was led to contact the pastor of Ken's church to arrange a meeting. Have you ever thought, *Lord, are You sure I am the person for this job?* I Googled the church's information and I got the office phone number and called for an appointment. Now, what was my plan?

What can I say? I was out of my realm and out of my comfort zone! I had made the call. I had made the appointment. I was in my car and sitting in the parking lot. I was full of insecurities and wondering if I should go through with it. I thought about how foolish I might look by speaking of these spiritual things. What if this pastor had been praying for help? Was I that help? Sometimes you just have to stop thinking of the "what ifs" and jump! I gathered my strength from the Lord and went in to meet with Pastor Matt.

If I had a plan, it was to stir up faith in the supernatural activity of God as I talked with him. With caution and anxiety, I revealed my unique spiritual journey. I told him about the experiences the Lord was sharing with me. Not all denominations and pastors are open to a charismatic spiritual life. I was treading lightly to see his reaction. He responded with an ever-increasing positive affirmation, and I began to relax.

Laboring Hard with Little Fruit

Pastor Matt was a very hardworking man. Our conversations were two-way. He shared things that were happening in his life. I opened up and expressed the experiential side of my Christian walk with Jesus. Frankly I was impressed with the dedication, commitment, and hours that he spent in pursuit of building a stronger Christian community in this church. He strived to excel in the men's mentoring and discipleship program. He labored many hours and spent a lot of one-on-one time with the men in his congregation. Yet he shared his frustration at the small amount of fruit he was seeing. It didn't take me long to see the downward trend that he and the church were in.

As part of the bylaws of this church, the pastor was given three terms by the board. At the end of each term, the pastor was evaluated before they would enter another agreement. Pastor Matt was concerned about going before the board for his review. He felt that his performance and hard work had not elevated the church. In fact, he was struggling to maintain what spiritual life they had, and it may have actually declined. If Pastor Matt wasn't at the bottom of this downward spiral, he was certainly near it. Isn't that just like God to bring help when our cries are loud and from deep in our hearts? I could see that Pastor Matt and the church were in their winter season. I hope you can see the irony here. Here was a spiritually vibrant pastor who had done the hard work of rising up in the spiritual ranks of leadership. He had endured the humbling of God's storms and trials. Now he was nearly fruitless, and he knew it. It is devastating to a pastor when they have labored hard and long with little fruit to show for it.

Pastor Matt and I met a total of three times. I eventually explained to him that the Lord had shown me a restricting demonic spirit that was hampering his work. It was almost as if I could see the wheels turning in his mind. This is not a typical subject to be shared, especially with a stranger. Yet he seemed to entertain the idea because of the difficulties he had been experiencing. However, it came time for us to end our meetings because it was clear to see that I wasn't meant to become involved with the church. I asked if I could pray with him and for the church. He agreed.

God's Intervention

Whenever I pray, I try to look inward to see what the Holy Spirit might be guiding me to pray for. So as I prayed, I would lift up all those things that He would bring into my mind through my thoughts and feelings. Sometimes I see images to help direct me to an issue to bring before the Father. I remember praying for this church. I was asking the Father to forgive any sins that had taken place within the church, on the ground on which it sits, and any corporate sins committed by the leaders or the members of the church. It was when I was praying for God to open a window to heaven above this church that I saw it!

I saw a picture of the church and how it sat on the grounds. I had my eyes closed as I normally do in prayer. I saw myself outside the building on the north side of the church. I was closer to the building than to the street at the property line. My neck was bent, and I was looking up. To the right was the church's steeple. To the left was the east end of the building and a fenced play yard for the children with mature shade trees scattered about. In the bottom portion of my view was the shingled roof of the church and the sky above it.

The sky above the church was covered with heavy gray clouds. In the center of the gray clouds I saw something equivalent to a pin piercing the clouds that were directly above the center of the church; in a circular motion, immediately the clouds receded in rapid motion. The church was exposed to the open sky above, and now it was lavished in wonderful sunshine. No longer was the church under a cloud covering. I was utterly amazed! As I ended my prayer, Pastor Matt prayed, and when we were done, I shared with him what I had seen. He was very gracious in receiving my prophetic observations during our prayers. There was little response beyond that, and I certainly don't blame him. Pastor Matt quickly brought our meeting to a close and off I went.

Back in my car, I felt that my mission was complete although I had more questions than the day I first approached the pastor. I got a chance to see how God ordered me out of my footsteps and used me as an intercessor for this church and for Pastor Matt. This was definitely a learning experience. I did like this adventure, and inwardly I hoped God would use me again—just not right away. I was glad it was over. I had pushed myself beyond my comfort zone. I learned that when you are being obedient to the Holy Spirit, rewards can come in various ways. As I drove off, I placed our meeting back in the capable hands of the Lord and moved on.

Chapter 3

A Second Visit

Isn't it odd how things enter and exit your life? Our lives had been enriched by attending the Christmas program at Ken's church. I am glad we said yes to his invitation. I thought my meetings with Pastor Matt went well. I saw he had accepted me and my "different" spiritual walk so my fears of rejection had not materialized. I stepped back into my regular routine of seeing Ken at work. We would often talk about spiritual things, and I always enjoyed seeing him. Seasons came and went and life settled back to normal.

Spring is my favorite season of the year because that is when new growth takes place. The trees bud and grow leaves, plants sprout up and blossom into beautiful flowers, and flowering trees explode into God's work of art. The fresh air is scented with the newness of life through the flora around. It is my life in the Midwest on the Great Plains of America. The warm temperatures have been long anticipated through the long winter days.

It was six months since I had seen Pastor Matt, and something inside of me was stirring to attend a regular Sunday service at his church. I talked about it with my wife, and we agreed to go one Sunday in May. I mentioned to Ken that we were coming back for a visit. The broad smile on his face conveyed his happiness. This time, instead of feeling unfamiliar and a little nervous, we looked forward to returning to his church and seeing our new acquaintances. It was a beautiful, warm Sunday, bursting with sunshine and a gentle spring breeze. The grass was a deep green, and the trees were full of leaves. The church windows were cracked to allow the spring scents to flow into the main sanctuary.

Pastor Matt greeted us as we walked in the breezeway. His smile conveyed that he was genuinely happy to see us and me in particular. I was relieved to see things were okay, considering that we ended our talks so abruptly last year. We walked into the sanctuary and found our way to our seats.

I could tell things were different from before. The worship team was already in place and within moments began playing their instruments and leading us in worshiping the King. The spiritual atmosphere of the church had changed—it was sweet with the presence of God! The people were responding with hearts of praise. What was going on? It was a complete turnaround from before!

My heart was light and engaged in the open heaven the church had become. I noticed that there were about three hundred people in church that day. It was three-quarters full. There was an increase in attendance. The spiritual emptiness was now gone, and the sanctuary was filled with spiritual life! They had moved from spiritual barrenness to blossoming and flowing in the living waters of the Holy Spirit.

It was somewhere in the middle of the service when it happened. Without warning, I saw a picture flash in my mind. It happened so quickly and was filled with such vivid description and color that I was shaken by it. I said a quick prayer: *Lord, what did I just see?* And, bam, there it was again. I saw it a second time.

Snapshot Image

Are you a camera buff? Have you ever opened the back of an old SRL camera? A single reflects lens camera? If you open the back of an SRL and activate the shutter, you will be able to see the aperture function. An aperture has a center point of opening in an outward fashion that varies in speed from one second to as fast as one-thousandth of a second. From the center pinpoint, the aperture opens, spiraling outward until it is fully open and then quickly closes. This allows light to hit the film within the camera in order to create an image. That's what it was like for me. An image instantly flashed into my mind so quickly that I was taken aback by it. I had been totally engaged in the church service. Then suddenly I was totally engrossed in interpreting what I saw. I was seeking the Lord, looking inward to an understanding of what had just happened.

Don't you love God's creative abilities? The picture I saw was a three-hundred-and-sixty-degree view. I don't know how, but I saw an image of the front of the church, the direction I was sitting in, and a complete image of the sides and back of the church's property—all at the same time. Maybe that is why I was so shaken. I had never seen anything like it before, so it was difficult to process. This is what I saw: In a surrounding image I could see all four corners of the property at once. Standing at each corner of the property was an angel! This church was now under angelic protection. I had forgotten that was what I had asked for when Pastor Matt and I were praying together. In the prayer two things happened. Not only had the cloud opened over the church, but now it had received transfer of ownership and was under angelic protection. I had forgotten about praying for the angels to be stationed upon the property. Today, in vivid detail and color, I saw it in the image God gave me.

He Already Knew

I was so distracted by these events that the service was basically over for me. I was anxious to talk with Pastor Matt and waited on pins and needles. Pastor Matt exited the service first so that he could greet the people on their way out. He would share a kind word or caring thought with each of them.

I was bubbling over with excitement as I told him about seeing the angels on the four corners of the property. Pastor Matt asked me a question that shocked me. He asked, "Were the angels looking outward?" "Yes, they were looking outward, with their backs toward the church!" The angels were protecting the church and his ministry against all evil.

Over the last six months since we had met, he saw the dynamic of his church change. I had a phone conversation with him later that week.

He told me that when the atmosphere of the church changed, the light of the Gospel impacted the people. There were people who became uncomfortable with the increased presence of God, and they left the congregation. On the flip side, people who were seeking the presence of God were being drawn to Pastor Matt's church and started attending regularly. The church had entered the spring season of a new life, a new breath of God was upon them.

This was my first experience of being used by God outside my own life and family. On a very limited basis, I had been shown things for my home church before this, but this was new and exciting work for me. I had grown immensely during this adventure. Being stretched is always hard, and the risk of looking foolish is unpleasant. But the Lord was leading, and I am glad that I followed Him. It made me spiritually hungry for more, and it increased my faith. Even though these were the challenges, I enjoyed them.

What Did I Learn?

I didn't realize it at the time, but the seasons of intercession I had gone through in my life were now bearing fruit. To intercede for a pastor and his church and bring change to their spiritual atmosphere was something the Lord had showed me way before this happened. I didn't understand it back then. Sometimes, when there were deep storms in my life, I would think to myself, *When will this be over? How do I cooperate with the Holy Spirit to help it be as short of a storm as possible?* Helping Pastor Matt was the firstfruits of those years gaining intercession.

I have read the book entitled *Rees Howells, Intercessor,*[1] which my sister recommended early on in my journey with Jesus. She could see the gifts emerging in my life. Reading about his life, I gained the understanding that a Christian can go through seasons of suffering for the purpose of being able to pray for a person, place, church, region, or even a nation. God responds by breaking bondages and strongholds, bringing about a transfer of spiritual ownership. When a season of trials begins, the Lord will show you what it is going to be applied to. Then seeing the results in action will bring you joy and satisfaction.

Learning is an ongoing process for me. It has been many years since my meeting with Pastor Matt, and I am still gaining insights from that experience. Within his church, a tradition had crept in, increasing in importance and usurping God for first place. It became more important than God to have their programs and traditions. I marvel at how this happens in our human hearts. As far as I am concerned, it is all too easy for this to happen. Those subtle changes bring us down a path away from the divine order of God's plan. People tend to forget to keep God first. I hope I am clear that I am not faulting anyone! We live on earth, which is a spiritual battleground. We strive to stay the course and grow in the ways of God. We can then fulfill the Great Commission. It is an ever-present vigil to walk in the fullness of Christ.

Another principle at work was the cloud covering over the church. The heavens were bronze. The prayers were bouncing off the clouds and not reaching heaven (see Deuteronomy 28:23). I have come to appreciate a place that abides under an open heaven. It is wonderfully rich in the presence of God, and awesome spiritual activity flows from it. In such a place, the Kingdom of God impacts lives and the people are saved. The Holy Spirit is pouring out His elements to Christians.

A very important thing happened at Pastor Matt's church. There was a transfer of ownership of the land!

> *"If my people, who are called by my name, will humble themselves and pray and seek my face and turn from their wicked ways, then I will hear from heaven, and I will forgive their sin and will heal their land"* (2 Chronicles 7:14).

His angels now stood guard, protecting the activities of the church. Ministering spirits aided Pastor Matt in proclaiming the Gospel to this area, and people were drawn to his church. They came without invitation postcards. The Holy Spirit was drawing people to the light and truth of the Bible. I had come to realize that the stirring I had initially experienced at the Christmas program was the prelude of the Holy Spirit.

I am learning to trust and follow Him. I can be used by God in bringing change to others in those seasons of deep trials and storms. Paying a price and being willing to allow God to change me from within has brought benefits to the Kingdom of God and joy to my heart.

Chapter 4

It Is All About Keys!

I am going to deviate from the natural progression that would lead us to the "new ministry" I described in the previous chapters, interceding for a church. It is important to open this new topic, the spiritual realm, and take a look at the dynamics of intercession that I am going to reveal.

One of my favorite Scriptures is:

"I know the plans I have for you declares the Lord. Plans to prosper you and not to harm you, plans to give you hope and a future" (Jeremiah 29:11).

Part of God's plans for my life was to help me understand generational cycles. I have found this topic to be surrounded with different points of view and at times it is downright controversial. Regardless of how people feel about generational cycles or the sins of the fathers, it is my life journey and I need to follow God. He has placed me on this path for freedom and learning.

At this point in my life, I seldom talk about my past. I have spent a lot of time and effort to be disconnected from my youth. In most cases of childhood abuse, the impression of the family dynamic is portrayed as normal. This was the same with my family, but it was anything but normal. To those of you who come from an abusive background, you would understand the phony appearance that was built to ensure others would see us as being a normal family. But within my own heart, my spirit told me something was wrong. However, we all played this game. Eventually, I would come to the position of just not listening to my inner voice. My thoughts were crying out that this couldn't be the way normal people live their lives. So I lived harboring internal conflict.

Looking into the Brokenness

What were God's plans for me? I wanted to learn what the health of Christ's likeness looked like. I wanted to comprehend what sin did to ruin relationships and a person's life. I had to identify where the breakdown occurred and connect it to the proper Scripture. I wanted to be able to assess what was happening in the spiritual realm because of sin and bridge it from the past. Only then could I see if it was still touching the present. It has been a compelling journey of connecting the dots. Looking inward at my own brokenness and the pain associated with it wasn't just challenging—without God it was impossible.

Each time God asked me to delve into the memories, I said yes. I was allowing God to do the work that He had in mind for me. The Lord introduced the molding and shaping of my new life in preparation for the ministry He had planned for me. The way God taught me these things was no less astounding than any other spiritual adventure He had placed before me. In the quest of understanding the dysfunction of my family, I joined many of the self-help groups organized just for that.

With each group, I achieved knowledge and freedom. I learned the "how to" of applying Scriptures to my everyday living for a healthy life. God opened my eyes to what happens when sin enters a person's life. It was interesting to see how a family can be impacted by sin and the effects those sins had within that family for generations. I came away with knowledge that I use today in seeing where people's lives are located on a scale I call the "Debris Scale."

Before I explain the Debris Scale, I want to share with you my greatest discovery. This was worth all the time and costs associated with my journey. When I took the time to look inward and apply all that I have learned to understand the effects of the sins I had in my life, I saw it. This one sentence has changed my perspective on my life and my feeling toward myself. Now, as an adult, I can understand the culmination of the journeys that the Lord had set before me to walk and the reflection of the prior three hundred years of my family's history.

I was born into a family line filled with so much dysfunction, it seemed there was no way I was going to come out of it okay! It was not normal, not healthy, but a life filled with loss, trauma, and pain. It had nothing to do with who I was or who I am. But I understood the litany of bad decisions made by those who went before me. My ancestors opened very bad doors in the spiritual realm, leaving a wake of destruction for all those to inherit who followed.

This brings me to my life's Scripture:

> *The thief comes only to steal and kill and destroy; I have come that they may have life, and have it to the full* (John 10:10).

The Debris Scale

To describe my model of the "Debris Scale," I will illustrate with a graph. The graph I have built will be on the negative portion of the scale for obvious reasons. Every human being is born into original sin.

Sin enters a person's life:
- After the age of reason it is not forgiven automatically.
- The effects of that sin remain, the destruction of healthy living occurs, and evil has its impact.

The deeper the sin, the lower the number is on the Debris Scale. The story in the Bible of King David and Bathsheba illustrates just what happens when sin enters a family (see 2 Samuel 11:14). King David's sins flowed into his marriage, then into his children and then into his kingdom (see 2 Samuel 13).

Take a look at the graph on the next page and we will build on it from there.

The Debris Scale starts off at a negative 1.

-1 On this level, negative one, you have those who are good people that are making bad/ungodly decisions but have not opened the door to deeper sin. They often live by a religious standard without having a personal relationship with Jesus Christ.

-2 On the negative two level, you could imagine a person having substance abuse problems, but they still function in society. They are caught in a web of sin, moving in a downward direction and often spiraling out of control. The substance abuse consumes provisions that are meant to flow into the family to meet their needs.

-3 On the negative three level are those people who have opened the door to abuses that destroy the spirit: sexual abuse, emotional abuse, physical abuse, and so on. It is serious sin for themselves and those who are the victims. This is not a one-generation problem! This flows down the generational line.

-4 On the negative four level are those people dabbling in the occult who choose it as a religion. They develop their skills in connecting to evil forces. It is in direct conflict with Deuteronomy 28. The result is receiving the consequences of forsaking God and pursuing other gods (see verses 15 to 68).

To summarize the Debris Scale:
- -1 Living a moral standard of life without God
- -2 People involved in substance abuse but still functioning in society
- -3 Sexual, physical, emotional abuse opening the doors to serious sin.
- -4 A person who practices the occult.

Are you curious about where my family fell on the Debris Scale? I discovered my family had practiced witchcraft on the Isle of Skye in Scotland.

Bridges

Building this bridge, I have to use a lot of concepts, and I need to add a few more. Church leadership can sometimes get into sin, and it opens the door for corporate sin. I was a member of a church for several years that had slipped into corporate sin (my opinion). The history of this church was built on a foundation of evangelism. Coming from their Scandinavian culture to America, free to practice Christianity openly, they were soul winners! It was common for the men to witness in the local taverns in hopes of bringing others into God's salvation. Seventy-five years later, it had slid off that path into becoming an ethnic social club at its heart rather than being a church that was serving Jesus. They had lost their first love and priority. What was once a daughter to the Bride of Christ was now a Christian community social club with little spiritual life left. I am not trying to be critical. Yet in my six years of being a member, the Lord had showed me His intent for the church to come back to its roots, but it just didn't happen.

The next concept I need to introduce in this arena is interceding for others in our walk with Jesus. In its simplest form I put intercessors into two groups. The first group is comprised of Christians who pray and intercede before God for others. The second group is made up of those who go through seasons of storms and trials to gain an intercessorship to be applied as God directs. A book on intercessors was my first exposure to this gift of God. Through it, I identified the seasons that I was going through at this time in my life with that of gaining intercession for others as God led me.

The last piece of information to share is Isaiah 57. This chapter in the Bible became a Rhema word from the Lord for my life. So many times and in so many ways the Lord brought this Scripture to me that I finally decided to dive into the meat of the Word and see what the Lord wanted me to know. Bible commentaries are a great way to gain insight into the Scriptures. I read many sources on Isaiah 57 and spent a lot of time seeking the Lord until in my spirit I felt I knew beyond a shadow of doubt the message He had for me. It can be summed up in Isaiah 57:14.

And it will be said: Build up, build up, prepare the road! Remove the obstacles out of the way of my people.

It was time. The Lord started to put all the pieces together for me. It was the season for me to begin interceding for others. It had begun. My spiritual lessons were to help me gain knowledge as a vessel of the Lord and use them to help others. This brief description in this chapter took the better part of ten years to learn. I had no preconceived thoughts about this education of spiritual principles. I was just trying to survive all the challenges and change I was encountering. Keeping up with the learning curve left me exhausted and my head spinning from the stretching it took to teach a simple guy like me to grasp the dynamics of it all. Then the fun part started.

Lock and Keys

Keys! I stated earlier that my secular profession is being an elevator mechanic. I have loved this job. All the talents the Lord has given me really come out in my career. He has brought out the best in me through working in the elevator trade. On rare occasion, when someone on my service route will drop something into the elevator hoistway, the item falls from between the doors and lands in the elevator pit. The outside door or hoistway door at each landing has a piece of metal we call a "sill." The elevator door inside the cab also has a "sill" holding the car door in place. The distance between the hoistway door sill and the elevator cab car sill is a minimum ¾ of an inch and at the greatest distance 1¼ inch. This is called the runby. My point is this: What are the odds of something falling through the door sills (located on the floors) and into the hoistway, descending to the pit floor?

During my workday, I meet with the building's liaison, which is the first requirement upon entering a building. If anything special needs my attention, the liaison will let me know.

One day I heard, "Hey, Tom, someone dropped their keys into the pit of elevator number thirty. If you have time, would you please go get them?" In order to access the elevator pit, I must run the elevator to the upper floors and pop the hoistway door open. Sending the elevator upward and away from my position, I opened the hoistway door with a lunar key to stop the car at a safe distance from the bottom floor. I then block the door open with a wedge tool and flip the emergency stop button. Next, I place a barricade in front of the door, reach into the hoistway, and grab the ladder to climb down to the pit floor. All kinds of things end up down there, but keys don't happen very often. A charge nurse at this hospital had lost her keys to the drug cabinet. She was desperate to get them back. What is the most common question from people when they see I am down in the pit? "Hey, is there any money down there?" If I say yes, they will then say that they had lost it a couple of days ago. Not!

Over the next several weeks, nearly daily I was being asked to retrieve keys from a pit somewhere. My route is fifteen miles across, so whether it was on the west side or the east side, I was retrieving keys for people so they could turn the locks in their lives: in the car, apartment, home, medicine cabinet—there were all kinds of keys for locks keeping things safe or keeping things locked away from view. For the next four weeks, not only was I retrieving keys for people who were waiting for them, some were standing by a phone waiting for my call to come get their keys!

Finally I got called to go over to Trinity Hospital on the east side. The sole purpose of this callback was to rescue a set of car keys for an employee so they could go home. I entered the building and walked down a long corridor. There was a woman standing there waiting for me. It had been a long, hard day for her, and the last thing she wanted to do was be detained. To her I was the key man! She was filled with appreciation when I handed them to her; she bounded out of work and on her way. I hope you are able to see the spiritual application here. When people get into sin or have generational sins in their lives, they need someone with the spiritual keys to help their lives move forward in Jesus Christ. Removing the obstacles is what Isaiah 57:14 said to do.

Unexpected Mentor

Being open to the Lord enables us to follow the Holy Spirit as He takes us from place to place in our lives. I was invited to attend an anniversary church service by one of my Christian friends. I accepted the invitation and walked into church a bit late. The usher walked me in to a full church! I walked up the side aisle to the fifth pew from the front and could feel every eye on me as we went. Wouldn't you know it, isn't our Lord humorous? This was good training for me to get over my "front-of-church" phobia. Within minutes, an elderly lady was called to the podium to speak. Shock of all shocks, she was talking about keys! It all happened so fast my head was swimming. When new concepts are brought to my mind, it is real work to get these old brain cells to develop new pathways. I needed more information.

Did you ever want to raise your hand in a crowded church to ask that question burning in your heart while four hundred people sit there quietly? How was I going to get to this woman for some one-on-one time? I had all kinds of thoughts running through my mind when her mini-sermon ended. The pastor stood up and thanked this mother of the church, and she quietly slipped out the back door leading downstairs. *Now how am I going to see her, Lord?* I asked Him quietly in my heart. I was so compelled I got up, hoping I wouldn't be noticed. I walked to the back of the church and into the vestibule. To my surprise, appearing out of the stairway from the basement was my new teacher!

For twenty minutes, out on the front porch and main door of the church, I grilled her for information. "Explain to me again how these spiritual keys work!" Over and over she explained the application and it started to fall into a completed puzzle. All the pieces, ten years of learning concepts, foundations of Scriptures, family reconstruction, debris scale, Isaiah 57—all of these were downloaded into my comprehension. I saw it! I was to use the spiritual keys the Lord has taught me to bring freedom for His children. I would pray with people, identifying their keys (sins or generational sin), retrieve them from the pit, and by the power of God, they would be set free! Wow!

Baby steps were needed! Starting out using spiritual keys took me the long way around. At first, I applied the keys to my family and friends. Then I moved on to those whom God brought to me so I could minister to them. I would interview a person for information on their family line. I wanted to understand the problems they were experiencing in their lives and relationships. This took hours! One item at a time, we prayed for and asked God to break off the effects of sin. We were closing doors to evil and bringing a new start—His plan for their lives. It was encouraging to see the immediate spiritual relief and change. This style of gathering information was wearing me out. *There must be a better way,* I thought. I went through all the people in my immediate life—*now what, Lord?*

Reaching Out

With God, there is always a way! Stirring up within me was a desire to have a pen pal. When I was young, the idea of a pen pal piqued my interest but it wasn't practical. So I put that idea on the shelf. Now with the Internet, the world was wide open for me to connect with people. Australia, halfway around the world, seemed like a good place to start. I Googled "Pen Pal," and wow, I wasn't ready for all the choices available. The question was, "Where do I start?" Christian Pen Pals seemed like the best choice, and I started the process to connect with another person. However, I was more into the idea than the other people on the website. I did connect with a deacon in a small church on the eastern coast of Australia. It was very interesting to hear about the movement of God "down under." Shortly after it began, it ended, and my pen pal idea was a bust. However, I learned a new skill and branched out to Christian chat rooms.

Christian chat rooms were a whole new environment for me. I was so green and totally unskilled in this arena, and it really showed. I quickly found out that I was not a "chatterer." All Christian chat rooms had a prayer room. Now this I could do. I quickly joined three or four Christian chat rooms and set up shop in the prayer rooms. Some prayer rooms were more spiritual than others. In the spiritual prayer room, people would come in, men and women, and start a rolling litany of praise and worship. Member after member, line after line, they lifted up praise and worship to our Lord and King. It was truly uplifting. Within all rooms was the ability to open a one-on-one window to speak to another person in a private chat. Here was where I continued using God's spiritual keys. On regular occasions, I would type a line in this room asking anyone if they needed prayer. About one out of four times, someone accepted, and within private windows I would minster to them and identify their keys. I would then bring it before the Lord in addition to their requests and needs. This was great fun. For a few hours each night, I would log in to a prayer room and wait for God's appointed time and person. The stage was set—everything was about to change!

I love our God! You cannot imagine the depth to His creativity and ability to introduce new things into our lives. My heart is filled with awe and gratitude for Him being in my life. There are new adventures around every corner, new growth opportunities day after day, and new levels to be gained. It is wonderful to walk in this spiritual life. I had no idea about the new ministry just before me.

What Did I Learn?

What did I learn about the keys? This was an incredibly hard lesson for me. There were many events taking place with retrieving keys from the elevator pits. Now I was to use them for His children. They needed to move forward and return to the life He had planned for them beyond the hindrances of sin. I had spent years understanding generational sins. As the Bible explains it, the sins of the fathers flow down several generations and affect a person's life. I first learned my own family background. Hours were spent laying out timelines and events leading back to Scotland and the clearances that took place in the 1850s that affected my lineage. From there, I spent three years dealing with traumatic events we had in our lives growing up. This helped me to get a fresh look at it from my adult perspective. It was in this group that I could see the effects of sin, the different levels of sins, and how sin affected the person, the family, and all others it hurt. I began to see important building blocks that were missing from a solid personality and family structure. I came to my own biggest personal discovery, which I shared with you before. These lessons along with my years of learning about dysfunctional families were now keys I see readily in people's lives, and as the Lord directs, I apply these keys to help others.

Let me add that the wind of the Holy Spirit blows where He wills. There were times of prayer in the Christian chat rooms when people would feel the power of God come on them during our prayer times. Of course, there were those who didn't notice anything! God knows the hearts of those people I was praying for. Those hungering for more of Him didn't go away empty. This was a season, and it was going to come to an end. A new season with new adventures was just on the horizon.

Chapter 5

An Open Heaven

We are still in the grasp of winter. It is totally dark by 4:30 p.m. and even earlier on a cloudy day. Life in the winter months is the perfect time for an "inside ministry." Our computer room is our third and smallest bedroom. We have a large corner desk on the north wall and a lounge chair across the room positioned just right for the wide-screen monitor. From the comfort of the chair, we can watch Internet TV and videos. We have two bookshelves in opposite corners that hold reference material to aid in the interpretation of Bible symbols. There are also several books on dream and vision symbolism. This is my window to the world, dispatching prayers and caring for those people God brings across my path. I have to give credit to my wife. She brought out the best features of my love of travel and made this a very comfortable place for me.

Dreams and visions from God are a big part of my life. There are those mornings when I will say to my wife, "Honey, I have news!" During the night, the Lord gives me information to aid in His work here on earth. I never know when this might happen. This is like the concept of a radio: A radio can only broadcast what it receives from the radio station by way of radio waves to the speaker. Dreams and visions from God only take place when we receive the information via the Lord. Most nights I prepare for sleep with my nightly prayers and then with an invitation. I invite the Holy Spirit to come and visit me during the night.

What happens when your head hits the pillow? Most nights within minutes, I am in a deep sleep. Other nights, when I can't turn my thoughts off, it can take hours to fall asleep. One night in particular, I was in a light sleep when I felt the presence of the Holy Spirit come upon me. Suddenly my spiritual eyes began to see while my earthly eyes were still closed. At first, it was as if I were watching white clouds parting and rolling back from the center of my sight. Layer after layer of clouds parted and disappeared off to the side. Then to my shock and surprise, a face appeared not more than four feet away from mine. I was really unnerved. I have learned that if I am fearful or resist, most times the vision disappears. I am beginning to discipline myself to stay in the moment so that I can see it through to whatever it is the Lord has for me.

What helped immensely was the expression on the face that was looking at me—it was beautiful! In human terms, this would apply most of the time. This time I need new words to describe the embodiment of the face before me. Gorgeous, stunning, divine, angelic—all are inadequate words to express the character of the facial features of the being in front of me. It is beyond my ability to tell you how beautiful this face was. I could not tell whether this face was male or female. I am at a loss of earthly words to construct a word picture so you can see what I was seeing. The expression on this face was telling me a message that almost audibly said, *I know something good that you will be finding out soon.* After we looked at each other for a few moments, the face began to fade away, not in distance but in opacity, until it was gone.

Then appearing in the same position as the first face was a second angelic face. It was just as beautiful as the first face and totally unique. It held a similar expression of knowing something good, and then it too faded from my view.

A third face appeared. It was as beautiful and unique as the other two with a smile and an expression of delight in our introduction. A fourth face then materialized before me. I was meeting a group of angelic beings! I couldn't keep up with all that was going on. I was stunned with information and experience overload. My head was swimming, but the best was yet to come.

Have you seen the movie Abyss? It is a sci-fi movie released in 1989 that tells a story of aliens living in the depths of the ocean. Slowly the characters in the movie encounter them. In one scene, the aliens use sea water to coalesce into a body of fluid that enters their subterranean sphere where the underwater drilling is taking place. This is to make contact with the people within. Now, do you have Internet availability? If you do, go to Google Images. Type in: "Movie The Abyss," and on the opening page you will find pictures of a likeness I am about to describe to you.

After the fourth angelic face disappeared from my view, from over my left shoulder came a stream of water flowing toward me. When it was about four feet in front of me, it turned to the right. The front end of the stream stopped there and began to form into a face. We were then face-to-face. I was in awe of the creative moment as the forehead emerged and then the eyebrows. The chin rounded out and the cheeks, nose, and lips were created. The facial features were complete as the cheeks lifted in a smile, and I recognized the warm expression as that of the Holy Spirit. The newly formed face had masculine features and fondness in His expression. He too conveyed a message of good things to come. I enjoyed this time and was fully relaxed and unafraid. I connected with Him and in my heart I didn't want this moment to end. As with the others, He too faded from my view. The clouds rolled back in, and before long, the spiritual presence withdrew, and it was over. At the end of this visitation, I had time to feel the depth of love and support it brought to me. I lay in bed stunned. (You should know that I didn't see the movie Abyss before this event happened. I saw it years later.)

New Ministry

I was profoundly impacted by this vision. I lay in bed memorizing and savoring every detail of the vision. Within days, I knew something was different. This is how it began. I had started an online prayer ministry by becoming a member of several Christian chat rooms, as I mentioned before. Within the chat rooms are several types of rooms for chatting. I would frequent the "prayer rooms." In here, the focus was on prayer and praise, and often people would come in seeking a person to pray with them for their needs. Right after this experience of angelic visitation, I entered a prayer room and asked if someone were in need of prayer. A woman replied. We entered into a private window (a one-on-one window where no one else in the prayer room could see our conversation), and she conveyed her needs for her family. I began to pray.

> Dear Father, I lift this person up to You now. I ask that You cover her with the blood of Christ from the top of her head to her feet. I ask that You surround her with Your protecting angels—any ministry of angels she may need.

> Now, Father, I ask that You please forgive her forefathers for the sins that they committed and the pain it has caused You. I am sorry for the pain, Father; please forgive them. Now, Lord, I break off every curse, stronghold, and grounds upon her life, right now in Jesus' name.

Right then, something new happened. Power, spiritual power, began to flow over and into her from the top of her head downward. She was unable to respond on the keyboard. The presence of God was so strong that she was helpless under the power of the Holy Spirit. She summoned up some strength to write. She wrote that she was in tears, flooded with the presence of God and all that He brought in the encounter with Him. The love and joy of God had entered her room and life. I continued praying for her.

> Father, I ask that You open a window to heaven over her life and pour out provisions upon her and her family, without measure. I ask, Father, for You to release all of the needs she has and that You would do even greater things. Father, please place Your favor upon her and her household. Let Your favor go before them; be with them all wherever they may go. In Jesus' name I pray. Amen.

She didn't respond after that. I left the private window of prayer and saw her log out of the chat room. Later that week I learned of the time she had with the Lord, there in her home. I had left and the Lord had remained. The Holy Spirit and the four angels had entered her home and ministered to her as only God can. I learned in the days following that the dynamic of her family had changed. She found a new church, had a renewed interest in godly things, and they started attending church as a family. They had a new beginning—the old passed away and the new came in. It was through the chat room, over the next month, she told me of all the changes that were happening and the increase of blessings they were receiving.

Across the Ocean

Jim would join the prayer room in early evening in the central time zone. For him it was late at night. Jim lived in Glasgow, Scotland, and there is a six-hour time difference between us. One night, I was parked in the prayer room waiting for someone to come in. In my send window, at the bottom of the chat room page, I had a message already typed and ready to go. "Hello, glad you came in to chat tonight. Are you in need of prayer?" Jim was glad for the offer because he was going through a divorce and needed God's help and the support of others. Prayer would be a big help for him that night. Both of us entered a private chat window, and I began with prayer. I started out with the same prayer I had shared with the woman. When I got to the breaking off of curses, the Holy Spirit and the angels entered his room, right there in Glasgow! Their manifested presence brought a wonderful atmosphere of love and awe to his heart.

I continued to pray, and once in a while he would respond. "Tom, I can't see the keyboard! My eyes are filled with tears, and the joy and love I am feeling is wonderful." Again, as he could, he wrote: "I am compelled to lift my hands up. My hands feel like they are on fire." Power from the Holy Spirit flowed into Jim's life, and he later told me after I left him that for hours he and the Lord had communion together. His room at home had become an intersection of heaven and earth filled with love and awe of the Almighty.

Jim worked a regular job, but the joy of his heart was the worship group he was a part of. Shortly after his experience with the Holy

Spirit, his group started performing in courtyards and public squares, reaching out to the lost. The response from the people was very positive and many were saved. To his surprise, people started extending offers to Jim and his worship group to come and play and minister around his area. They were now spending more time in ministry and in evangelistic outreach and loving it all.

Celtic Calendar

During the investigation of my family history, I was doing research at the local library and asked the librarian to help me locate a book. As I was following her, I noticed a book sticking out of the bookshelf about an inch beyond the rest. It was at eye level on my left side. Walking past, I felt the Holy Spirit guiding me to grab it. I took it and kept following the librarian. It wasn't until after I got the books that I was originally looking for that I read the cover of the one that I had grabbed. It was titled *The Celtic Year*.[1] I quickly looked over the book, wondering why this one would have any importance to me. I reviewed the references in the back of the book. To my surprise, "Donnan" (my last name) was listed. Immediately, it had my interest. Further, I discovered that the patron day of Saint Donnan is celebrated on April 17. Reading the accounts of Saint Donnan during this era was like reading the book of Acts in the Bible. Signs, wonders, and miracles followed him wherever he went. In the history of Saint Donnan, I discovered that he planted churches throughout the Inverness of Scotland and settled on the Island of Eigg in 617. He founded a monastery there and had fifty-two followers. Eventually he suffered a martyr's death. There was a window of time when I was following in the footprints of those who had gone before me.

Details! Over the years, mostly in the beginning of my spectacular journey, I would keep a journal of events, dreams, and visions. I looked back into an early entry and found it. I had this vision on May 28, 2003, at 3:45 a.m. It was forty days after Passover. I looked for meaning to this event and found an article on the web with information that struck me. Forty days after Passover was when Jesus' ascension into heaven took place. On May 28, I was blessed to ascend into a new heavenly ministry.

At the time, I had no way of knowing this open window from heaven had a limited number of days. The frequency of encounters was happening regularly. I decided to buy a bulletin board, a map of the world, and map pins. I started to make small notes with the dates and times, descriptions of what happened, and how God manifested with the people I was praying for. Quickly I had colored dots and notes scattered all across the world. Anywhere in the English-speaking world, I could reach people, pray with them, see God move, and place a pin in the location of their corner of the earth. I was having trouble believing it! Pins were placed all across America, Hawaii, Australia, New Zealand, Canada, Norway, Berlin, and places beyond. The Lord was impacting and anointing in the Caribbean and northern parts of South America, as well. One astounding connection was in Spain. The Lord immediately turned an entire family in a new direction, answering a wife and mother's prayers.

On sleepless nights, I would get up and turn on the computer in the hope of connecting with someone on the other side of the world. I even tried to enter foreign language prayer rooms to see if someone spoke English but that didn't work well. I did get to connect with people during the night whom I wouldn't have come across during my daytime routine.

I would say I had between 150 to 200 pins on my world map. One of my favorite stories came from a missionary who was soon to return to the field in Africa. In one week's time she would be leaving Pennsylvania, and she came into the prayer room looking for prayer for her travels to the mission field and then prayer for her time there. We entered a private window and I started to pray. Soon in my window came a question: "WHO ARE YOU? I have had many people pray with me in my life but never like this! God is here with me and the love is so good." Well, I dropped back into the main room, and she logged off and spent time with the Lord in her home.

I ran downstairs, filled with excitement, and told my wife about what had just taken place. I then rushed back up to the computer to see if I could connect with another person whom God would bring across my path. Occasionally, someone would receive a healing in their body. The most notable was a seventeen-year-old boy who had a spinal cord injury and was paralyzed from the waist down. He said during my prayer that he could feel tingling in his legs. Within thirty minutes he told me he was standing. The next time we met online, in the prayer room, I asked him if I could talk with his mom. During this conversation with her, I believed God healed this boy. She took him to the doctors to examine him. Praise God!

The oddest story was that of a young man in his early twenties. He came into the prayer room and threw everyone else out. On a high horse, he stated: "Everyone not praying and not praising God, GET OUT." Over and over he did this until it was only he and I who remained. At this point, I wanted nothing to do with him. However, I had a push within to pray with him. Because there was no one else in the prayer room, I asked him if he wanted to pray and I began. Nothing could have prepared me for the visitation this man had from the Lord. It was very powerful. This is the only one that I remember where someone said they felt oil flowing over them in their spirit. Not only oil, but he stated he felt fire on his body. The presence of the Lord was strong and his room was filled with Him. You see, this young man wanted to be a worship leader and he was in school for this position. The Lord was anointing him for service unto Himself.

The feeling of making a difference in the world around me was something new that entered in my life. People's lives were being changed and enriched with each touch from God. I was able to pray with a woman from Christchurch, New Zealand, several times. She shared with me how much she appreciated how quickly the presence of the Lord would fill her room. She went on to say how dry the churches were in her region and how wonderful it was being in the presence of the Lord. Co-laboring with the Holy Spirit and the four angels brought a new sense of purpose to me and I enjoyed it a lot. I remained invisible and behind the scenes, and the entire focus was upon the Lord and how He was manifesting during His visitation with those whom I connected with in prayer.

Devastation Hits

Then on Saturday night, October 18, 2003, it all suddenly came to an end! I was devastated. I tried for a month and not once did anyone feel God's presence like before. Then the questions started. *Lord, did I do something wrong?* I prayed and sought the Lord, but the door was closed and it was over. I was no longer co-laboring with the Holy Spirit and the four angels I had been introduced to in May. I grieved the loss; my heart was troubled over the disconnection of those I had enjoyed working with.

Have you ever had unanswered questions of the Lord? Of course, I know we all do. Sometimes the blessed understanding is given to us at a later date and eventually satisfies our longing to know. As I got ready to write this account, after more than seven years, I was able to see more and finally know why the season came to an end.

Are you the kind of person who looks for all of the information and all of the clues you can find for the deepest possible understanding when it comes to the things God shares with you? Do you try to glean every piece of knowledge you can from the dream, vision, visitation, or word of knowledge you received from the Lord? I do! So as I started to dig into this again, I prayed that the Holy Spirit would guide me. Saturday, October 18, 2003, is a Jewish holiday, Shmini Atzeret. I Googled it and came across an explanation of this holiday. One word popped out in the first explanation: stoppage! Another definition of Atzeret is "final." And so it was. October 18, 2003 was the final day of working under an open heaven. I also counted the number of days from May 28 to October 18, 2003, using a date-to-date counter. I learned the length of the ministry was 143 days. Then, using a Hebrew lexicon, I entered the number 143 into it and the results were "glorious!" To say the least, it was "glorious" to see the hand of God moving upon His children.

I was in the thick of seeking people out to pray with in Christian chat rooms reaching around the world, and I found myself pushing forward with a driving force to reach people. I would spend hours setting up private chats for prayer and staying with the person until our time came to a close. I might be in prayer with a single person over an hour, before the time was right to leave them alone with God. It was getting hard near the end, but the joy of a person basking in the presence of the Lord drove me onward. I questioned myself on how hard I was pushing. At the end, I realized that I unknowingly was racing to see how many people I could connect with before the Shmini Atzeret came. I am glad that I had short nights of sleep. The evenings, weekends, and holidays were spent on the computer striving to be used by God and reach my brothers and sisters in the Lord.

Let me finish up with the following story. It was a Friday, near midnight, and often people would come in at that time because they could sleep in on Saturday. The rest of their households were often asleep, and they could be alone on the computer. That night, PK came in for prayer. I could see PK was female, and I said, "PK is a usual chat name?" She told me, "PK stands for Preachers Kid!" She was desperate. Her life was filled with spiritual pressure and pain. In adolescence, PK had been abused by a stranger. She was struggling with a fractured spirit and all that came with her trauma. She was hurting and was earnestly seeking God for help. God had connected us. Having come through the healing of abuse in my own journey, I understood and knew how God's tools could bring healing. As we prayed together, a compassionate God rushed into her room. He wrapped His loving arms around her, cut away all the ungodly cords, healed the fractures, delivered her soul from the trauma, and lightened her soul. She said, "I feel so much lighter now and the pain is gone." Even now, tears fill my eyes as I remember how God stepped in and touched her in just the way she needed. She is on a new road to living life free from the bondage of sin inflicted upon her. Thank You, Jesus!

Chapter 6

Redirection

I have always been drawn toward life-changing, credible books about people who have experienced our supernatural God. What is it about these books that feed my hunger in connecting the dots for my own life? I can identify with their experiences relating to the Trinity. It is an intimate knowledge one gains only through participation. As I read these books, the natural outcome in my life is the validation.

This morning, I read the first chapter of the gospel of Matthew. In Joseph's account of his dream, he is directed by an angel not to release Mary from their betrothal. He knows that this is no ordinary dream but an intersection of two realms. The spiritual and the natural realms come together and encapsulate him. For Joseph, this experience is life-changing and dramatic just like the waking experience of Zachariah, the father of John the Baptist. The only time Zachariah ministers before the Lord in the Holy of Holies, he meets the angel Gabriel. This encounter is life-changing and forges the family path for his son, John the Baptist. Can you see the redirection of both of these lives and families after a divine encounter? What I want you to see is the disruption of our natural environment by the visitation of heavenly beings and how shocking and moving it is to our bodies, minds, and spirits.

Testimonies of Heaven

Currently a very popular book is *Heaven Is for Real*.[1] The absolutely amazing part of this book is the indisputable accounts of heaven given by an innocent little boy, Colton. His serious illness, at age three, introduces his heavenly experience as he lies between living and dying. To his parents, Colton's illness teetered on ending his brief life, but God answered their prayers. It wasn't until months later that Colton started to share with his parents the knowledge he had gained in his heavenly experience and the people he met there.

Another book I enjoyed was *Akiane: Her Life, Her Art, Her Poetry.*[2] The sovereignty of God is a mind-boggling concept. Why did God intervene in the lives of this family? That is a question I will never know the answer to. This little girl didn't have a serious illness nor did she hang in the balance between heaven and earth. She had a visitation from the divine and was given extraordinary talents. The result of her visitation ushered in a personal God to an atheistic family and brought about an abrupt change in their spiritual beliefs. Unbelievers became believers in Jesus Christ as the Son of God through Akiane's divine encounters. Her gift was the gained knowledge that she received. This is nothing less than a miracle. The redirection of her life and that of her family touch many people through her art and poetry. Her life helps us to see the existence of an intangible God.

Searching to Know

Faith is the bridge that connects us with a supernatural God. Skepticism comes easily to the nature of man born in original sin. When it comes to the prophetic gifting, credibility is the first step to receiving the knowledge that will help in hearing a word or message from God. How do I begin to believe in a visitation, beyond a shadow of a doubt, before I share it with others? I have a spiritual identity crisis!

Everyone in the world has an opinion about God. We are made to explore a supreme being. It is in our DNA to search for His existence. Once we seek Him with our whole heart, mind, and soul, He is faithful to bring us to His plan of salvation. When we receive Jesus as our Savior and Lord, skepticism doesn't end immediately. Let me make a jump here. In the prophetic, it is all about hearing from God. It is just as undeniable as the exchange in Joseph's and Zachariah's experiences.

To complicate things, there are two applications to the prophetic: the Old Testament and the New Testament. We all need to have this clear in our hearts and minds.

It is like translating something in English into another language. I have been learning to translate God's symbolism into a message to share with others for twenty years. Most people reading this book have read or heard Scripture verses from the book of Revelation. I love the description the apostle John makes in describing a flying scorpion that shoots fire. Today, we would call those flying scorpions Apache helicopters. Get my point? I need a prophetic professor, so to speak to help me interpret. Where do I go? Who can I find? I need someone who is prophetically credible. I need someone with whom I can really talk.

Pastor John Mark Pool gave a prophecy that no person in their right mind would give unless they had an inside source giving them great confidence. In January 2005, John Mark shared with the world that New Orleans would be flooded and under twenty feet of water. Bold, brave, and confident was he in relaying God's message. Of course, we know the truth as history now, but it wasn't at the time. Here is the credibility that I was looking for. How could I get to meet him? (Just so you know, John Mark is considered his first name.)

Pastor John Mark Pool is a teacher, speaker, and author. The thought entered my mind to seek him out. I again Googled his website. Located at the bottom of his webpage was his itinerary extending out several months. Although he and his wife lived in Louisiana, his current itinerary was all up and down the East Coast. To me, this was not close enough for me to want to travel to meet him. However, he would be in the Cleveland, Ohio, area and that was only six hours away by car. Road trip! I signed up for the conference and training classes being hosted by a pastor in Wickliffe, Ohio. This three-day course was held September 14-16, 2006. It was my opportunity for a breakthrough in believing.

Let's Look at the Timeline

• January 2005: Pastor Pool gives his prophecy concerning New Orleans.

• August 29, 2005: Hurricane Katrina hits the Gulf Coast with disastrous effects. During the storm, several levees that surround New Orleans break, and can no longer keep the waters back. Parish after parish is flooded. Although he stated it would be the French Quarter that would be under water, I have come to learn in a vision, seeing the French Quarter undisputedly gives a geographic location. The name of the city was given as a whole by seeing the French Quarter. However, the French Quarter was spared the worst of the flooding. Why is all of this so important?

• January 20, 2006: I had a life-changing vision.

I needed to make the transition to have complete confidence that I was hearing from God! So, let me tell you about my road trip to meet Pastor John Mark Pool.

I wasn't one to take time off from work to travel to a conference. If one was convenient, within fifty miles of the house, I might go to it. This day, however, I swapped cars with my wife for the long journey. Her car is more comfortable and the one that we use for long trips. I don't travel on the Indiana toll roads all that often. It has been years, maybe even decades, since I had driven on these concrete ribbons.

The Indiana toll roads had been revamped. Now, at the point you enter the toll road you get a card pinpointing the place you entered the system. Information upon the card will show you the required toll when you exit. No longer do you need to stop and pay intermittent tolls. It sped up the process. The freedom that I felt traveling down that road was exhilarating: leaving my responsibilities behind, living in the moment, the weight of working and day-to-day living left behind.

Six and a half hours later, I was approaching the Cleveland skyline. Cleveland's downtown area gives a view of the lake as its backdrop. Hard to drive and sightsee at the same time. Riding past the downtown area of the city, I headed for the suggested place to stay for the conference. It was a newly built motel with a block of reserved rooms for the speakers and guests. By four o'clock I was checked in, unpacked, and ready to go eat before the opening meeting.

I get nervous if I am not on time. The directions from the motel to the church were very good. I was early by a few minutes. I checked in and moseyed over to look at the display of books they were selling. I was impressed with the large volume of prophetic authors. I don't think I bought one; I needed time to think about it.

The evening began with praise and worship. The pastor really got into the worship. Then came time the introduction of Pastor John Mark Pool—the man I had come to meet. He stands six feet tall, one hundred and ninety pounds, in his mid-fifties, sporting a mustache and goatee. Just a bit of gray hair, enough to show his age. I had no preconceived notions of what I expected him to be. But I didn't expect him to be the way he was. He was an educated man who told us about his life and how he worked for many years in the business world. He spoke to us in common-man language and I found him easy to listen to. I felt both comfortable and uncomfortable. I know that doesn't make sense. He could be me, if I were a speaker. I saw the possibilities. It scared me and I became uncomfortable, but I also marveled at the potential for my life. We are nearly the same age.

As he spoke, it was like confetti falling from the sky. Pieces of my prophetic life began to fall into place. This would be the beginning for me. Enough pieces fell into place that I began to glimpse the picture that the puzzle contained. There was some additional element to his life, however, that I couldn't quite put my finger on. His style of teaching was clear from the beginning—he taught from experience, using applications that I could easily grasp. He was not a weirdo, the profile of a stereotype the world might give a person of his faith and spiritual gifting. Here was a man I would be proud to emulate in my spiritual walk. You might be surprised that I was one of only fifteen people who signed up for this training. Someone was covering the costs that far exceeded the money brought in by the registrations.

At the conclusion of our first night of teachings, I hoped Pastor John Mark would take the time to mingle with us. It had occurred to me with so few people I might get some one-on-one time with him. When I introduced myself and told him where I had come from, a smile spread across his face. He understood I must be hungry to learn if

I had driven several hundred miles to hear him speak. At the close of our conversation, I extended an invitation to him for breakfast. He balked at first but then said if I could wait until after ten o'clock he would be available. "Sure!" I said. I understand the demands of ministry. Even though he was on the road, there were still articles to write and people to call. There were schedules to make and remake for the days ahead. I learned later from eight to ten o'clock in the morning is his time set aside to be in communion with God each day. His first priority of the day is time alone with God. This left a lasting impression on me.

More Than Food to Eat

Together we walked into Bob Evans, my favorite pancake restaurant. The hostess brought us over to the booth across from the walkup counter and we settled in. I had my sights on my favorite meal combo, and the waitress took our order. Now it was time for small talk. My technique was to start with an ice-breaker leading to more in-depth conversation. I was there to get prophetic validation. I talked about my experiences and visitations, and I know that there was questioning in my tone of voice. He picked up on my uncertainty. As a teacher sees into a student, he heard and saw the hand of God upon my life and got to the chase. He told me, "Tom, trust in God and relax. Stop your fretting and begin to step out in what you are shown by the Lord." I worry in my efforts to be concise and accurate. But how am I going to progress without taking chances?

During our time together, he shared with me new information about a crisis pending in the spiritual realm. He was risking by sharing this with me. This allowed me to grow by example. I learned he is not a loner when it comes to his dreams and visions or prophetic impressions. He shared with me that he is connected to a group of prophetic people who share things together. I mean, when a person in the group gets a "word" from God, he would document it and send it off to the group. The group would then reply with their insights, observations, and level of importance. In other words, he gets their feedback. This is something I didn't have in my life at the time. I was learning a new outlook on this gift from God. I was grateful to him. He was speaking into my life and helping me learn. I greatly valued my time with him, and it ended all too soon. At the end of breakfast, he was off to do more work. I was off to do some sightseeing.

Sightseeing and Digesting Time

I drove past Wickliffe looking for a place to see Lake Erie. Even though I was on a shoreline road I couldn't see the lake. A senior citizen center fit the bill. I parked and ventured over to Lake Erie, one of the five Great Lakes. I sat down upon a rock close to the water's edge. Scanning the horizon, looking over the surface of the water, I saw water as far as the eye could see. It is much like Lake Michigan but instead of running north and south, Lake Erie goes east and west. Twenty percent of the world's fresh water is right here resting in the shorelines of our Great Lakes. Sitting here, looking inward and feeling my love for God, I questioned Him. I was rerunning this morning's dialogue with Pastor Pool through my thoughts. *Lord, what am I to learn? How am I to change?* There was more to come before the time for prophetic coalescing began. Time passed quickly as it does when I am in communion with the Lord. I scanned the beach for just the right rock. My wife was starting a rock garden and what better time to find a treasure and bring it home for her.

Back at the motel room I had time for a nap. Just as I was drifting off to sleep, I heard a sentence being spoken. There was no one in my room, and I quickly noted this was spiritually happening. This is what I heard: "Tom, I am going to give you five minutes." Okay, this doesn't happen to me, this type of experience. This was new, and what in the world did it mean? I didn't have to wait long to find out. At the opening of the service, after praise and worship, Pastor Pool called me up front. For five minutes he prayed and prophesied over my life. What a gift and the beginning of the redirection in my life.

The conference was a pivotal event for me. Meeting Pastor John Mark Pool validated my prophetic walk and that was why I went. He talked about his life and one such story was of his near-death experience. In great detail, like that of Don Piper, author of *Ninety Minutes in Heaven*,[3] he (John Mark Pool) shared with the group his trip to heaven. I centered in on the conversation he had with his dead brother who met him there on his arrival.

In his story, it was his brother who reminded him the reason he was on earth: You are to give the Word of God to the world, hence "Word to the World Ministries."[4] This was the word given to his mother and it was his commission received early in life. He received a life's redirection in this encounter, and it was in this experience that the love of God entered his life. That was the missing element I talked about earlier. While in heaven he was immersed in the atmosphere of God's love, and it has changed him forever. During the conference, moving from one person to another, he released love into their lives, and we all drank it up. He later went on to write his own book called *Path of a Prophet*[5] with an in-depth account of his journey to ministry.

Chapter 7

Clipboards

Change! How well do you cope with a changing world or the changes in your life? Living as Christians, we hopefully see that change is a regular part of our spiritual walk. I was just at a Sunday night service, visiting a local church. The outreach was called "Hearts Ablaze," with two guest speakers. As the second pastor spoke, he revealed a truly transformed life. In his chosen profession before knowing Jesus Christ, he had robbed banks! Really! Pressures, guilt, and the weight of sin brought him to a saving knowledge of the Lord. Standing before the church sharing with all of us, he spoke of the transforming power of God. You could clearly grasp that he was a new creation born of the Holy Spirit.

I was inspired and encouraged; this former bank robber, now pastor, invited people to come forward for prayer. He asked, "Who wants to be used of God in our community and wherever the Lord may lead you to serve Him? Come forward for prayer." All but two people went forward to receive an impartation from God. This step of faith was a clear statement from all those who went forward. They were saying, I am available to You, Lord. Use me! I could see all this happening from my seat in the rear of the church. I did not go forward myself.

God puts us through the Potter's Wheel, which is the molding and shaping process. Knowing the power of prayer, especially by those empowered by God for change, I didn't go forward. I was right in the middle of all the change that I could handle at that point. Once we make a heart decision to God that we are available for Him to use us, job specific training begins. The training begins by peeling away our old nature. Next is the developing and depositing of God's nature within us. In this journey we are then placed to become Christlike and transformed into His image. Wanting to be used by the Father God, daily I look for those encounters and divine appointments. These are life's little adventures that I have grown to like. My status with God is "available"!

The world is a big place. It is no challenge for God when He wants to bring together two people for His plan and purpose. Think about the apostle Paul! In a vision, he saw a man calling for him to come to his location, Macedonia (Acts 16:9).

To this point, serving the Lord had always been within the confines of my family, church, and community. These areas were all I had ever known when it came to ministering to others. I have shared with you how the Lord used me on the Internet to minister as well. I never had to leave the Chicago area, or to us natives, "Chicagoland." I was so surprised when it became clear that I was being called to go to another city in another state.

Hearing the Voice of the Shepherd

Quickened! It had not been a word in my vocabulary nor had I ever heard it until I started to learn to walk by faith and not by sight. Quickened is defined as a "to become more active, sensitive." I was learning that when the Holy Spirit wanted my attention during the regular day, He used this technique. I would be quickened in my spirit to notice something. For example when I have been reading the Scriptures, there are times a verse hits me in a new way. Suddenly I stop in my reading, and the verse seems to leap off the page into my awareness with new insight and meaning. Quickened!

Okay, I'm giving you some groundwork here on how I was moved out of my routine. The Holy Spirit was teaching me that when something in my ordinary life happens several times in succession, then within my spirit I am quickened to it. I then have learned to start asking questions. *Holy Spirit, You have my attention on this issue. Now, what am I to learn or do with it?*

The following is a story that I would like to share with you concerning my adventure toward connecting with people. I was about to meet several people whom I didn't know who were located in cities where I had never been before. It was in a string of events that I am quickened by the Holy Spirit to pay attention. The end result was a new adventure.

Divine Connections

Being an outside contractor, I have a service area and many long-term customers. This particular day started like any of the other days in the past twenty-five years. In day-to-day work, I maintain their elevators. Today, I am quickened to clipboards!

I am at the largest account that I service. It is a large trauma hospital, two blocks long and one block wide—Ken's building. Easily, I walk up to five miles a day there. At every turn, I am finding a clipboard. Clipboards are for attaching paper to and then writing on while on the move. Starting early in the day, I find empty clipboards in the oddest places. One clipboard was resting on the elevator pit floor as if placed there. Another clipboard was neatly placed on the desk in the machine room (secured and seldom entered without authorization).

I started keeping track of each discovery, and before noon I had counted four. The afternoon was no different; I continued to encounter clipboards. The final one of the day came when I was walking up a stairway in the northeast building of the complex. It was at the top of the landing, and it was the seventh clipboard. *I surrender! Lord, I am convinced that You are trying to get my attention with all of these clipboards.* This had never happened before. Before if I wanted a clipboard, I couldn't find one. Now at seven different locations, in five connecting buildings, clipboards were lying unattended. *Lord, what am I to learn or understand about all these clipboards?* He would soon begin to show me.

How I Go About Seeking Him

Before I share what He showed me about the clipboards, let me explain how I go about seeking Him for His wisdom. I like reading about the visions that the Old Testament prophets had. I was just reading Amos yesterday. In chapter eight, the Lord asked Amos, "Amos, what do you see?"

"A basket of ripe fruit" he answered.

The Lord then went on to explain to Amos what He was about to do concerning Israel. To me a basket of ripe fruit wouldn't convey that the destruction of Israel would be on the way! But it was. My point is that I always need to seek the Lord. I need to think outside the box and be open to the Holy Spirit's communication. I need to glean information pertaining to His quickening in my spirit to see and hear His message. Clearly, trying to understand what the message would be concerning clipboards was going to be outside my normal realm of thinking or my common experiences. Where should I start?

I am very analytical. This is my common approach to solving problems. Far too often it gets me frustrated, and I wind up spending a lot of time searching. In this case, I allowed the Holy Spirit to guide me. After several hours He brought me to the Internet—and it was an intensive search. There I discovered "OpenHeaven.com." In the "Prophecy Forum," there are people who will post an article starting a thread! What's a thread? Glad that you asked! I was really dense when it came to understanding this Internet concept. This is when I learned that you could share your thoughts about what a person had just posted in their article (prophetic words). A discussion is then started. The discussion continues to roll on and on, person after person, exchange after exchange, becoming a thread! Let me tell you how I came to this site.

I was doing research for a pastor on prophetic websites. At the time I found all the clipboards, just in front of me was a divine appointment. I came across a site that had a prophecy forum. All visitors could read the posted articles in the prophecy forum—and this is worldwide. However, if you wanted to join the thread, you had to join the site. After prayer and seeking the Lord, I joined the site and began to post comments on the articles people were sharing in the open forum. I don't know about you, but I was a nervous wreck coming out of the safety of my protected life and allowing myself to be vulnerable in this new way. I had stepped out of the metro community that I was used to. All of a sudden I was in a world community where all English-speaking people entering this site could interact with me. I was challenged to grow by my new experience. I had to know my Scriptures. I had to be confident and strong in my own position of faith and my walk with the Lord. I treaded lightly at first until I grew in confidence of my ability to convey my thoughts in the thread forum. I began to post articles and even started my own threads. I would then interact with those who had responded to my post with encouragement or help for their challenges. In the following months, I became friends with several people. Here is the point: in order to post an article, often you must first copy your texts to a clipboard, and then transfer it to the site's article forum.

A word of warning: the Internet is a place of great risk to people who are not authentic and not to be trusted. Even on a Christian website there are people not to be trusted. Great caution is required. I never gave out personal information, and I always took steps to secure my privacy.

Months went by and I was sharing with others the things the Lord was showing me through dreams and visions. I always struggled in the understanding of the symbolism that the Lord showed me. Just like the example I stated earlier of the vision Amos had with the basket of fruit—knowing what the message the Lord intended for me to understand was paramount. Once I had a grasp of the treasures within, I first applied it to my life. Did it fit? Then, if the answer was no, did it fit for anyone I knew? Did it fit in with my church? Did it fit in with my community?

This time, I had a vision about a church and the removing of the effects of sins. Not only did I see it for one church, but I saw it for a second church, and they were both connected. I was stumped! I was about to enter into a new ministry, interceding for churches in another state, and none of the pieces for this puzzle were coming together.

What Did I Learn?

What did I learn from the incident with the clipboards? Do you remember when you first started using a computer? There were all new terms and programs you had to master. You tried to take the information and put it into practice. For example: "cut and paste"! Well, that's what it has been like learning about being quickened by the Holy Spirit. I was starting to learn new terms that would be applied in the spiritual realm.

Of course, when I am quickened (that doesn't happen every day), it distinctively stands out. Let's just say, I needed help to learn this lesson so that my senses would jump to high alert. I would turn my thoughts toward the Holy Spirit and focus inward. In time and prayer, through a series of events, I would come to an understanding of how this dynamic works. Then I would start praying for the application of the information that was brought to my attention.

With the clipboards, I was at a loss in the beginning, just plain stumped. However, I was already doing research on prophetic people. I was looking for those with a proven track record by examining articles they had written. When I found someone who was prophetically reliable, I would contact them by e-mail. This was in the hope of connecting them to the pastor whom I was working with to develop the prophetic website they were building at his church. Ultimately, I came across a prophetic site at www.openheaven.com, as I stated earlier. It opened up all kinds of new contacts for me.

Three new people would come into my life through this website. I didn't know at first that Pastor Pat and his wife, Sue, were only going to be a one-time encounter. I would soon travel to their church according to the Lord's divine timing. Through the message of clipboards, the Lord used me to help a church in a new city. The next person whom I would be connected with was a pastor to impact an entire region.

Chapter 8

Being Led by the Holy Spirit

The Holy Spirit has been my tutor in learning to minister to others. From one lesson to another He has taught me. Because of Him, I have been gaining spiritual ground. From one hands-on experience to another, I was moving upward. I followed Him as He led me. The funny thing about learning and lessons, it is hard work and there are always new things coming out of left field to surprise me. The prophetic forum brought me to meet several people. Often at that website, I found there to be pastors and their wives, both posting articles and sharing with others in the forum. They were contributing in the ongoing threads people would post. This brought me to become friends with Pastor Pat and his wife, Sue, who live in Tennessee.

Pastor Pat and his wife were new to the prophetic forum, like me. We found we had similar views and common interests in the Lord. To explain an important component, this website had a staff of overseers who were involved in the articles and postings. They helped all members to keep a clear standard of the Christian principles held by the founder and to keep those posting articles and contributing threads to remain in line with the site's purpose. It was good to have the constant interaction with the staff. They provided challenges to points when they noticed someone didn't seem to be aligned with sound doctrine and scriptural application.

This is a common problem within the prophetic arena. I believe they used this method as a teaching tool for people who were new to it all. To identify the staff, they had a marking of "Admin" alongside of their name. When you joined a thread or posted your own article, your name, a chosen picture, and a token appeared, stating your rank and how long you had been a member on the site. I always got nervous when an "Admin" would join my post and enter the thread to be part of the discussion on different points. Talk about being stretched!

Remember, even if you weren't a member, you could still read the posts. It was hard enough for me to take a dream or vision full of spiritual symbolism and turn it into a message/article. In the beginning, it would be frustrating for me to get people to see the spiritual application of the article. The staff would see the confusion and enter into the thread to bring clarity. I was grateful for their help. A good part of being involved with this site was that people from all over the world would come in to read the posts. Through the entries, they could see how God was moving in the prophetic community and what He was saying. On occasion, a person who was seeking God for a word or a prophecy could get a Rhema word from the Holy Spirit by reading these posts. For those new to the word *rhema*, it is when the Holy Spirit will take a scriptural word from the Bible to the general population and make it personal for you.

Case in point:

"For I know the plans I have for you," declares the Lord, "plans to prosper you and not to harm you, plans to give you hope and a future" (Jeremiah 29:11).

A rhema word for you in this Scripture is when you receive it for your life by the direction of the Holy Spirit. In the forum, people would connect with the words posted and would be touched by the message.

Now back to my new friends. Working full-time, Pastor Pat was on the website only occasionally. However, Sue was on the website daily and that is who I most often came across in threads and articles. Pat, Sue, and I exchanged personal e-mails with each other so we could communicate outside the forum. For me, finding other prophetic people was a big help.

Follow the way of love and eagerly desire gifts of the Spirit, especially prophecy (1 Corinthians 14:1).

I can remember the place and time when I prayed to receive this gift. From my heart I determined to be open to the Holy Spirit and please God. By pursuing this gift and being open to it, I could be a blessing to the body of Christ.

Dreams and Visions Forum

A second forum that I was part of was the dream interpretation forum. People would post their dreams, starting a thread, asking for help in understanding what the Lord's message to them might be. Because of my active dream life, I learned when dreams are my own or when they are dreams through which the Lord was communicating to me. There is a distinct difference, and my intent was to help people see the difference. Pat, Sue, and I often partnered in addressing people's dreams to aid them in seeing messages being given to them by the Lord.

Dream interpretation is hard work for me! I always say I understand about 65 percent of what I am shown in them. I like to know beyond a shadow of doubt the meaning the Lord intends for me to see. So for the better part of ten years, I bought every Christian book I came across to help me. I have spent hours seeking additional insight and lots of time in prayer. If you are gifted with dreams and visions, you know how hard it is. It truly is like learning a foreign language, with a twist of personal knowledge and background added in to make it relevant and unique to each individual. It probably would be funny if I asked my kids about those earlier days. I have scared my kids half to death warning them to watch out for this and that over the next couple of days. "Be on your guard!" I would tell them. I thank God they aren't nervous wrecks as a result. I would see my children, in great detail, in a car accident or other of life's difficult events, not realizing how to interpret the symbolism. Converting spiritual symbols into an earthly message has been a long journey.

Note of caution: People with the verbal prophetic gifting are very different from those with the visual gifting. For them, the heart of God, through the Holy Spirit, flows into their hearts and is spoken through them. This is to edify the Church and uplift His children. This is why I believe people from all over the world would come into the forum. They wanted to be lifted up by an encouraging prophecy.

Pat, Sue, and I would help people with their dreams. In a tutoring application, we hoped to shorten the amount of time needed to see its meaning. During this time in my life, to my surprise, a new window and a new realm of dreams began for me. Stymied, I found that I was in need of help to interpret the new and surprising symbolism I encountered. I turned to Pat and Sue.

The following is a dream as best as I can remember it. I couldn't find it in any of my journal entries:

I'm in a church. It has white trim with dark maroon on the walls. The style of the church was rich in traditional Early American, like you might see in popular Southern denominations. To my left, off a bit, on a solid wall there is a white, six-panel door. It was striking, the white doorway with white trim, against the maroon wall. I was seated in an odd place for me. I saw myself seated in the front pew on the left side of the church. Traditionally in some churches this is where the pastor sits before going forward to deliver his message. The pews were made of oak wood and had a cushioned seat that ran the length of the pew, covered in maroon material. Stunned for a moment, I came to the realization that something was happening to me. I had become an agent for repentance. Flowing through me and out of me was the effect of sins! I feel embarrassed without even knowing if anyone knows what is going on. How could they? It was happening spiritually and without their awareness; however, I was feeling awkward. Then the dream ended.

A second dream happened immediately afterwards, and it was very similar to the first. I'm in a second church, very much like the first but different, and the same thing happens. The removal of the effects of sins flows through me, and the result is the church is as clean and white as snow. Then that dream ended.

Okay, I e-mailed this dream in hopes that Pat and Sue could help me because I didn't have a clue. Somehow, I was to help a pastor, or two pastors, with the effects that sin has had on their church. The reply from Sue was not what I expected. They understood it right away and saw that it was their church in need of God's help and that I was the person He was sending them to bring His aid. I was amazed! How in the world was I going to get there? I was being called outside of my region for the first time!

Chapter 9

Florida Bound

Everyone has experienced phone calls that come with shock and sickening effects. A loved one or maybe a close friend has had something bad happen in their lives, even something life-threatening! Ed, my brother-in-law, collapsed at work and was rushed to the hospital on a Wednesday. It was so serious I felt compelled to leave immediately and be with him. Flying was out of the question. After talking with my wife, I decided that renting a car and driving from Illinois to Florida would be the best way for me to go. Calling my boss for immediate time off didn't work out the way I had hoped. He said that doing so would be very difficult. Several other coworkers were taking time off already, and it would leave him shorthanded. He strongly suggested, very strongly suggested, I push it back to the next week. Silently, I said a quick prayer and said, "Okay," knowing I could leave right after work on Friday or early Saturday morning. I next called and set up a rental car. Then I called my sister to see how things were going.

Ed has been my big brother and mentor over the years. He brought me into the elevator trade. We worked side by side for several years. He is a mechanical and electrical genius, as far as I am concerned. Working with him taught me a valuable lesson in our trade. Ed said to me one day, "What would you rather do: pull hoist cables or electrical wires?" My first two years in the elevator trade were filled with replacement of the elevators' hoist cables! It is backbreaking work. Each cable has a series of steel wires gathered together with a set number of strands called a "lay." There are usually six lays, each having nineteen wires, or what we call 6-by-19 cables. Each cable has a hemp rope core for lubrication. Most elevators have around three to eight cables in all, keeping the cab suspended in the hoistway.

An elevator is designed to be suspended by only the strength of one cable. All additional cables are to increase the longevity of their life span. Cables weigh hundreds of pounds, as determined by their size and length. Electrical wires are so much lighter and usually concentrated in the machine room and controller area where the work is easier. Working with Ed set my career toward the electrical direction of the elevator world. With Ed as my mentor, I set out to better learn my troubleshooting skills and ability to comprehend the functions of the controls rather than the mechanical portion of the trade.

I have a rich history with my brother-in-law. And suddenly he was teetering on the brink of death. It was hard to wait. Ed's blood levels were extremely low and that's what caused him to collapse. But what caused his blood volumes to be so low in the first place? Tests were rapidly ordered, and they quickly found a tumor in what is called the ileum portion of the colon. It had grown to six inches in length and was bleeding. Ed was slowly bleeding to death, and this had been taking place over several months. He was losing blood faster than his body could produce it. Upon the discovery of the tumor, an operation was scheduled for Friday. The procedure was a success, and Ed was then taken to the recovery room. He was extremely weak from this ordeal and susceptible to immune system infections. That was a big concern! What we learned later is that only five percent of people who have this type of tumor survive! Most unfortunate people who have this die before it is ever discovered. It was by the grace of God that Ed is still here today. He is a living witness of the mercy of the Lord.

On Saturday morning I was in my rented car, headed to be with them in Florida. If you are like me, twelve to fourteen hours of driving time is my max, and then I must stop for the night. The Best Western in Macon, Georgia, was my target, and I was really tired by the time I arrived. The delay in my departure, due to my boss wanting me to wait, actually helped me out. I knew the outcome of Ed's illness by now, so I wasn't an emotional basket case while driving to see him. It was working out.

There have been a lot of relationship losses in my family. My parents are both with the Lord now. My sister Sandy passed away young at thirty-nine years old. My grandparents are deceased, and many of my aunts and uncles are gone too. I would have been at my wits' end if it wasn't for my relationship with Jesus. I had the confidence that He was with me and watching over Ed and Sheila. It did make a big difference to me.

Death Had Happened Often

I was twelve when my mother died. My youngest sister and I were not allowed to see her in the hospital before she died. We didn't have the chance to say our good-byes or tell her we loved her. We did not hear her last words of guidance and that last "I love you" from our mother. More importantly, we weren't able to hear what she might have wanted to say to my sister and me. It was lost forever. I regretted that turn of events that was made by those older and wiser than us. Missing those moments was a cost too huge to calculate. It sent my life down a road that no one could have imagined.

As a child of twelve, it seemed like my mother left the house one day and never came home. I have never said this before, but I always watched the mail thinking I would get mail from her one day. That was how it felt as a young boy. Oh sure, there was a funeral. But I was too young to handle her loss, and this fantasy was how I coped. Now you know why I was so compelled to be with Ed. In the same way I was compelled to be with my sister Sandy before she passed. I would never again allow a loved one to depart without being with them. When I finally arrived in Sarasota that Sunday afternoon, it was so good to see Ed's smiling face as I entered his hospital room. My sister Sheila was right there seated next to his bed to help him in any way. She was still shocked at how close they had come to being separated by death. It all happened so fast. I felt relieved in my heart when I saw the strength Ed had. The worst was over, and now we had reached the recovery part of the serious illness—and in this first week, I would be there to help.

Have you ever had surgery? Those incisions that the surgeons make to gain access to the internal organs become so sore and touchy during the healing process. The incisions don't like to be bent, stretched, or get wet, especially in the first few days. When Ed got home, he spent a lot of time recuperating in his La-Z-Boy recliner positioned right in front of the TV. I watched him as he slept, grateful he had survived. God is good! The La-Z-Boy was the only place he could find comfort and relief. Every cough brought a series of painful facial expressions, letting us see his struggle to get better.

My goal was to be his right-hand man. I was a gofer for his every request. Sheila needed the extra help to enable her to do all the other things a household requires. They were still raising kids. Grandkids are tough enough, but they had an even harder job—teenage girls. However, life must go on.

Ed and I watched TV to pass the time. I discovered something about him I didn't know before. He likes "judge" TV shows. We watched every judge show there was on the schedule. I could almost hear a gavel hitting the sounding block during my sleep because we had seen so many of these shows. I became a fixture in the house during that week. Even the dog was coming to me to let him outside.

Day by day, I watched how Ed improved. He had been given numerous pints of blood while in the hospital to build him back up, and it was working! Now at home, by Thursday I was convinced everything was going to be okay with Ed. Sheila didn't need as much help now that he was taking care of his own needs. For example, he was now able to get to the fridge. This is a big event for anyone recovering from surgery. By now I felt safe, that everything was going to be okay.

I made plans for my return trip home, intending to leave on Friday. I went to the computer room set up in their connected garage. Lots of people in Florida use their garage as additional living space. In the Midwest, in the winter, we would be a Popsicle if we used our garages like they do. Off into the garage I went to surf the net to find lodging in Tennessee. They had a dial-up Internet connection (can you believe it?) while I had the need for speed. Slow, slow, slow. I spent hours and hours looking for any hotel room in Knoxville, Tennessee, that I could find. There was a convention in town as well as a huge university activity. I could not find a single room available in the downtown area. I finally settled for a mom-and-pop lodge on the edge of town. Now, I needed to know if Pastor Pat and Sue were going to be at home.

Predestination

Pastor Pat and Sue were going to be at home, and they were very excited about my visit. I was able to make an appointment with them for 1:00 p.m. on Saturday afternoon. The stage was set. Oh boy, what have I gotten myself into now? It is one thing to send e-mail, but it is another to sit down and talk with people who are really only acquaintances. With two nights reserved at the lodge, I printed out the driving directions for both places, the lodge and the church. Pat and Sue lived in the parsonage on the church property. I had the address printed out on a MapQuest page and I was ready to go. The lodge was just a mere two miles from their church. I was set. Despite my wife's cautions about meeting people off the web, I was totally prepared.

I was comfortable with leaving Ed and my sister at this point. I just knew he was going to be okay. With kisses and hugs we parted, and I started my journey home by a new route. On this leg of the journey, I again had a sense of freedom driving down the road. I love to drive. It must come from my father, who was a truck driver. His left arm was always tanner than his right. I can see him now with his arm hanging out the cab window on warm summer days. Now, I was heading north to a town and place that I had never been to before. This was truly a new adventure for me. My mind was filled with thoughts of God and how He was going to use me to help this church. I allowed the Holy Spirit to fill my mind with images and ideas. Time flew by, mile after mile, through the open country, and it seemed like I was on autopilot as I drove.

Atlanta was a whole other thing. Have you ever driven through Atlanta? There are portions of the expressway where you only have a half mile to position yourself from one interstate corridor to merge onto another interstate. I had no copilot to help me now; she was at home. I focused my attention on road signs and switched lanes quickly so as not to miss my ramp. Despite these challenges, I liked driving through Atlanta; it was very pretty. A Southern city, newer than Chicago, it just had some intense interchanges to traverse.

Once I got to Chattanooga, it was all new terrain. I had never been this way before. Coming from Sarasota, Florida, it was a long day's drive for me to make Knoxville, Tennessee, in the same day. It was dark when I arrived. I couldn't see the landscape at this time of day, and that was a bummer. It was nearly 8 p.m. when I drove into town. It was a city filled with wonder, and I looked at the golden sphere lit up with all its lights donning the horizon. The downtown area looked clean and full of life. I love to travel and experience new places. I was dazzled by the Knoxville skyline. Still, it was unlike downtown Chicago; nowhere in the world is there a city like Chicago. But Knoxville was new and exciting and bursting with excitement and adventure. I checked into my lodge, drove around, and located the church for the next day. I was ready!

Unity in the Holy Spirit

The mom-and-pop lodge was a sleep-cheap establishment. After sleeping in, with no pressure of a schedule, I got ready and took off for some sightseeing. I spent the time before my meeting with Pat and Sue to get a feel for the city, spiritually speaking. I could probably write another chapter on the things that I learned and saw while I walked around town and met people. However, I'll to get to the point of why God brought me here in the first place.

Here I go again! Do you remember the first story of my contacting Pastor Matt in the beginning of this book and how I was out of my element? Well, here came adventure number two! I was looking at the church and the parsonage from the street where I had parked.

The parsonage was a nice two-story Cape Cod-style home. It was time to meet them. I walked up to the door feeling nervous and awkward. My knock on the door was answered in just moments by Pastor Pat.

At last, we were talking face-to-face and not through e-mails! Right behind Pat stood Sue and their little dog. I felt warmly received and before I knew it, we were in conversation and sharing life's experiences as if we had known each other for many years. In a short time, I felt myself relax as the conversation took many topic changes and covered an assortment of issues.

Being understood by our peers is a basic human desire. There I was, able to freely and openly share my prophetic experiences with two people who understood because they too walked in these things with God. One sad drawback of this gift is that there is a large amount of rejection that comes with it. I don't blame people. Seeing into the spiritual realm, experiencing the angelic and the Lord in a real, manifested way, is hard for most people to accept. I was like that at one time in my life. However, here we were, talking about our experiences in God and totally understanding each other. Stepping out and trusting God hasn't been easy. But now, I was feeling relieved. I could see now this was truly a God-ordained meeting.

A transition point took place in our conversation, and we got down to why I was there. Pat and Sue became transparent in speaking about the problems they were experiencing with their church. As a matter of fact, Pat had closed the church for almost two years at this point, waiting upon God to bring a new start. The church and its members had become so out of control, walking in sin without any acknowledgment of their sins. He had felt compelled to close the church doors. Repentance didn't seem to be on the horizon or an avenue for a godly upward direction. This is a pastor's worst nightmare. It resulted in many sleepless nights, heartaches, struggles, and unanswered questions, especially of why this had occurred.

I have known several pastors and their wives over the years. I never knew how lonely they can be in their ministries. It is hard for them to have close friends to talk to, especially if they are experiencing problems themselves. They don't have many places to turn when things aren't going well or when they are walking through deep struggles. I needed Pat and Sue to be open with me, and they were.

Reflecting back on the dream that had guided me there in the first place, I saw the actions I was to take, but not the details I would need to confess and ask repentance for. I got the details in their flood of emotions pouring out of their souls in the tragedy of a good church turned ungodly. Clearly I could see what part this information was going to play as I moved forward in ministering to them. It was a very hard road they had been on.

Closing the church didn't end the problems. They still received hurtful phone calls. Also, there were disturbing conversations from church members, and there were members of their own family who didn't understand the steps they were taking, nor the reasons for their closing the church building. It was ugly, but through it all they persevered. They held on to their faith and cried out to God for help. My heart broke for them. Truly it was the desire of their hearts to minister and share the Gospel with the lost! In their ministry they worked to teach and build up the saints for their edification. At this point they had been waiting for more than two years for this new beginning to arrive.

Supporting a Second Ministry

I didn't know it, but Pat and Sue had leased out their gymnasium, adjacent to the church, to a street evangelist. On Saturday afternoons, he ministered to the street people of Knoxville. This preacher went out with buses and picked the homeless up from the streets, shelters, and underpasses, and he brought them into the gym for food, clothing, and a church service. He too was a former street refugee. Having lost it all, his wife, children, home, and business, he lived on the street until Jesus brought him out of the pit of despair. It was when he was in the hospital, sick and malnourished, hanging on between life and death, that Jesus came into his life. Totally transformed, he is now full of love for Jesus. He scours the highways and byways looking for the down and out. He brings them to the church in hopes of introducing them to His Savior.

It was now 4 p.m., and the service started at 5 p.m. I had come to intercede for the churches. I felt compelled to begin the work that God had sent me to do there and I told them so. Sundown was not far away.

Pat walked me through the church that was adjacent to the parsonage. Immediately, I knew I was in the right place. It was a traditional sanctuary, with white wood trim and maroon-colored walls. The pews were covered with a material very much like the color of the walls. I was lost in the atmosphere and didn't hear Pat while he was talking to me.

Confirmation

In an instant I was back in the dream that had started this whole adventure. I remembered the presence of the Holy Spirit surrounding me as the dream began. So vivid were the images of the inside of this building. Everything seemed to flow in real time. I tried to keep up with noticing all the details so that I could to commit them to memory. Now, being here, it seemed like I had been in this building before. It was not an exact duplicate in its layout, but the colors and pews and the position of everything fit. It felt right!

Then we left that building and entered a breezeway that led to a school area with three levels. Pastor Pat told me about his plans of opening a prophetic school using this portion of the building to make classrooms. Next we walked back into the breezeway and over to where his office was located. He was spending a lot of time, energy, and resources to restore a large part of the building, and his office was almost complete. We stepped back out into the hallway, and as he led the way there was a doorway to another church.

In the origin of this congregation, the founding church had grown too quickly and a larger church was planned to be built. However, no one had the heart to tear down the beloved first church. So they let it stand and used it in several ways. And there it was just like in my dream! There were two functioning churches on the one piece of property, just as I had seen, symbolically, in my dream. The decorated color schemes of both church buildings were just as I had seen them. What a confirmation for me!

Time was now gone, and Pat needed to be in the gym. *What do I do now, Lord?* We had exited the church and were back out in the front of the gym where I met with the new pastor/street evangelist. There was a myriad of activity needed to set up for that night's service and the atmosphere was pregnant with anticipation of what God was going to do. Quickly I asked Pat if I could go through the churches, anoint them with oil, and pray throughout the property. Of course he said yes. Walking me back to the doorway, a side entrance, Pat unlocked the door, allowed me to enter, and then I closed the door. I was alone in the church.

Intercession

I had brought anointing oil with me, one of those highly scented oils, and as I was progressing from door to door, window to window, the sweet fragrance grew in the sanctuary. I started to pray that the Lord would wash this church as clean and as white as snow. I knelt on the first step of the altar area. I was pleading with the Lord to forgive the sins I had just learned about in my conversation with Pat and Sue. I looked inward to what the Holy Spirit was showing me to pray about. I prayed until I felt satisfied that it was okay. Then I moved on to the next portion of the church area, the classrooms.

This three-story portion of the building was lit with the daylight coming through the windows. Barren and cold, it was unheated and unlived in; it was cold in atmosphere. However, it had the promise of life to come, in a new beginning of the church that was so desperately desired. I spent a few minutes in prayer throughout the different levels, anointing the windows and doors as I went.

Eventually I returned to the breezeway, where I would turn and head to the office area and the doorway leading to the second church. This time, however, it was different. As I entered the hallway leading to the office, a cold chill passed through me. The hair on the back of my neck stood up on end. As I stepped forward, I saw an image in my mind of me flying backward, several feet above the floor and crashing into the wall of the church I had just been in. Something didn't want me to pray in this portion of the property. Not losing my focus, I continued on my mission, anointing the doors and windows and praying as I went forward, asking for the forgiveness of any sins.

Pushing through my anxiety at that time, I entered the second church. Here my actions and prayers were pretty much the same as they had been in the first sanctuary. I took the time to pray until I felt satisfied in my spirit, and then I retraced my steps to leave. I was exiting the side entrance and closed the door behind me. My work was done and now I was moving on to the next part, the evening service in the gym. I met up with Pat and Sue in the back of the gym, where the service was nearly ready to begin. I feel that it is necessary to say that at this point in my journey, this was preplanned by God for an appointed time. I was in the shelter of His wings, and I was not alone. Those who were with me were more than those who were against me. However, I have learned to make sure I do not step outside of the plans that God is leading me in. To do this it would cause me to be outside His covering and His protection for my life.

Pat and Sue introduced me to many people before the service began. I didn't know it at that time, having never done anything like this before, but I liked meeting people from different walks of life and different backgrounds. It was very exciting and new. Up front in the gym, where the worship band was set up, there were five musicians. They began to play songs helping us to worship our King. Things got hopping when they turned to the bluegrass-style worship songs. People started popping out of their seats, lifting their hands up high. They were being moved by the Spirit in the music that touched their souls— country home-style bluegrass. As they moved from song to song, the impact could be seen as I watched things from the back.

Pastor Pat couldn't contain himself any longer. He left the back and walked up the side aisle. I watched him reach into his rear pocket. Now my interest was piqued. What in the world was he up to? Standing in front of an open microphone, Pastor Pat withdrew something from his back pocket—it was a harmonica! He tapped his harmonica with both hands in preparation to play as if he had done this a thousand times before. His toes tapping away, he joined in with the worship team and stepped up the enthusiasm to another level. I loved it!

Did God bring this all together? Had God been developing me to minister to pastors and their wives with struggling ministries? To be an intercessor for them, changing the spiritual atmosphere of their churches? I didn't have a clue at this point. I was just following the Holy Spirit. I would learn the answer to this question in hindsight, plus there was more to come.

This is what I do want you to see from all that I have written in this chapter. It was Saturday, April 19, 2008, and Passover began at sundown! Today was their exodus from a church in bondage due to a long season of runaway sin. Today freedom from that sin has come, and a new beginning has arrived. Did God put this all together? Yes! Just think about it—my brother-in-law's sudden illness, my boss's insistence that I wait a few more days, and Ed's quick recovery. All of this led toward me being available to connect with Pastor Pat and Sue on the beginning of the Passover. I like to say: "God orchestrated all events to coincide with His plans." And that is something only He can do.

I contacted Pastor Pat and Sue right after I left, and the church had reopened its doors. Without advertising, twelve people came for the first service. Was it an easy road moving upward? No, it was not. But a year later when I called Pastor Pat, they had become an international ministry assisting in conferences to ministers from other countries. God began to open up new doors for them and new ministries! Praise God!

Chapter 10

Testimony of My Brother-in-Law, Ed

I have watched Ed battle cancer over these last eleven years. It has not been an easy road for him and my sister Sheila. Many times I have used the expression; "Ed, you have dodged the bullet again!" With each cancer reoccurrence, God has seen him through and brought more time to him here on earth. Below are Ed's words expressing each new discovery of cancer, his treatments, his surgeries, and his will to live for God and his family. However, this last occurrence has brought about an amazing transformation. It is a revelation to the use of our time here on earth. Whether it is looking at the end of our own mortality or the end of the age, time is short. Please read Ed's words and listen to his heart!

He writes:

In the year 2000, I had a mole removed from my upper left lip. It turned out to be melanoma, but they had made a clean cut and said I didn't need to do anything further about it. No additional treatment was needed. We had just moved to a rural area in Arizona, and I was busy working on our five-acre home.

In 2003, I found a small lump under my left jaw. It was a tumor in a gland, and three weeks later it was removed. It was melanoma again. This time I had radiation. They took out eleven nodes around it and they were clean. I went back to working on our place plus the little country church that we were going to. The church needed a lot of repairs, and so I had been working on fixing it up. It was my labor of love to the Lord.

In 2005, we moved to Florida to help with the care of my elderly mother. She was in early stages of dementia, and my sister, who was her primary caregiver, needed help. In my new surroundings, I found a good oncologist and continued to see him.

In 2008, he said I was now five years clean (cancer free), and he hoped he never saw me again. But that was not the case. I had been working as an electrical subcontractor. I love being busy. One day at work I felt I was having a heart attack. Whenever I would do any heavy labor, my chest would tighten and it was hard to breathe. I had no energy.

My wife made an appointment with a cardiologist. When he saw me he said that I was anemic. I told him that I had just had blood work done a few months before and it was all fine. He was so sure that he sent me to get blood work done ASAP. He said that he would probably be calling me to go to the ER for a transfusion. Within three hours I received that call. My blood count was so low that my body had started to shut down. That was why I couldn't do any heavy work. I received four units of blood that day. Then I entered a week of testing to find out why I was losing blood as I had no outward signs of blood loss.

Finally they gave me a small camera to swallow (to take pictures of my digestive tract and intestines), and they discovered I had a tumor in my ileum. This is between the small and large intestines, and it was digesting the blood loss. I was bleeding internally and didn't know it. I was shocked and surprised, having only just been released from the oncologist four months prior with a clean bill of health—cancer free. I had surgery and they removed the tumor and surrounding lymph glands. It was again melanoma. I went through half the treatments of chemo but had to stop. I couldn't stand how sick it made me and the pressure on my chest. After I was healed I went back to what I loved, working.

My wife and I were involved in a local church here in Sarasota. We went to church on Sundays and a small home group twice a month. I didn't join any of the men's groups or Bible studies. I went to church and I prayed at home saying my nightly prayers. It was hard for me to read my Bible as I have dyslexia. I knew God understood.

Then eighteen months later, they found a small tumor in the left side of my brain. In December, I was having severe headaches and my wife took me to the ER. They decided to admit me for a twenty-four-hour watch. While in the room I was administered a pain shot that caused a severe reaction. It took twenty minutes and at least five nurses and doctors working together to stabilize me. I was then put in a different room. They had to find out what was happening. I was told I was behaving like a stroke or seizure patient. I didn't know how to communicate or feed myself. I couldn't remember how to use the call button for a nurse. My wife stayed with me twenty-four hours a day for the next two days. When the surgeon's assistant came in two days later and asked me a question and I could respond correctly, they said I was going to have the brain surgery. The surgery went well. The tumor was removed. The operation had affected my vision and I lost my license to drive. Surprisingly, the recovery from my brain surgery was much easier than the abdominal operation I had had years earlier. Within weeks I was back at work.

I had follow-up care and was sent for an MRI three months later. They found that there had been a small sister tumor that had been behind the tumor they removed. It was small and the surgeon suggested I have a GAMMA knife (Cyberknife Radiosurgery non-invasive cancer treatment) to take care of it. So, I had this done in February of 2010. It was a very difficult procedure. When I had the next MRI about three months later, they found that the GAMMA knife procedure hadn't worked. In the meantime, I was feeling fine and went back to work.

We were now in our own home (we had been renting a house before), and we were having a small group meeting at our place. It was a real blessing and we had friends who were praying for us.

In June 2010, I was scheduled to have the next brain surgery. Our son had come for a visit to help me. When he and my wife took me to the ER with a 103 temperature, they thought I had meningitis. I had an MRI and three spinal taps. They couldn't find what the problem was that was causing the fever. I had complications with the fevers and headaches, and they still could not find the cause after bringing in various specialists. Finally my wife called a neurologist. She told him how I was doing on the steroids before they were discontinued and I started to decline and become sick.

He agreed and they decided to keep me on the steroids longer. I had an inflammation around the original surgery site. With the reinstated medicine, I responded well, and after couple of weeks we drove to Indiana and Illinois to spent time with family. I was weak but got stronger each day.

Then in late August, we flew out to Arizona to see our girls and several of my friends. We then went to Nevada, where my wife and I celebrated our fiftieth wedding anniversary. We renewed our vows on a riverboat with family and friends. It was a wonderful time. When we got back to Florida I went back to work. Everything was back to normal.

In late December 2010, I had another MRI. Can you believe it? I had another tumor. Aren't there times in your life when you put your face in your hands and cry out to God and ask "why?" This time the tumor in my brain was on the other side, in the cerebellum, very near the brain stem. I had a PET scan (Positron Emission Tomography, which takes 3D pictures) to make sure there were no other cancers.

In January 2011, I had yet another brain surgery. This time it was not the result we had come to expect. They got the entire tumor but found staining on the brain stem (bad information), and they are not giving me much time to LIVE! This was the first time in ten years that they were not hopeful.

I have gone through three brain surgeries for the removal of tumors, and now it has been two weeks since my surgery. I've really been looking back upon these ten years and how I have wasted so much time. I mean time for the Lord. I have been working with non-Christians all this time. They know I am a Christian, but I never laid out the salvation plan or gave my testimony on how Christ changed my life. There have been so many opportunities to share Christ with others, and I never stepped up to do it. I have peace with what the doctors have told us. I know I'm going to be with my Lord, and it will be a far better place. But to stand before Him (Jesus) knowing that I did not do my best for His Kingdom hurts my heart.

So my prayer, my cry, my admonition to all of you is, don't waste the time doing what you've always been doing. Ask yourself if you are doing what He wants you to do. Don't sit on the fence thinking you have time. No, you don't! You could die in an accident tomorrow and your time would be gone. If you are a strong Christian but don't feel comfortable talking to others about the Lord, then you have to trust in the Holy Spirit, and He will give you the words. We have to step out of our comfort zone and share everlasting life with others. We need to encourage people to grow in the Lord and to spend time in the Word (Bible). That's how we get to know Him more. That's where we find our strength to do what He calls us to do.

Today I stepped out of my comfort zone and off the fence. I had asked the pastor of my church if I could speak for a few minutes to the congregation about something the Lord had put on my heart. I had been praying about it along with my wife on what to say. When my pastor called me up front, my prayer was, *Lord, let it be You who will speak through me. Not in my words but in Yours, Lord.* I shared with them about how I've wasted time not doing the Lord's work. How we have to get off the fence as there are many who need to hear this message. I told them to seek God to find the strength to do His will. He will do it just as He is doing it for me today. If you are on the fence because you have questions about surrendering your life to Jesus or are not sure how to pray then seek help. Go to the pastor or to the elders or to the deacons who are grounded in the Word of God and ask them.

I am off the fence and I plan to tell others about the saving grace of my Jesus whether He gives me six months or six more years to live here on earth. My eyes have been opened to the call we all have, and that is to reach others for Christ. My prayer is that with the time He gives me that I will touch the hearts of others and they will want to know this Jesus who saves. That is my prayer for you, as well. If you are sitting on the fence, get off. You don't have the time you that you think you do. Don't waste it. —ED

In July 2011, Ed's illness was taking a toll on his health, and the doctor told Sheila he didn't have too much time left. So now what do you do? Wait to visit or see him while he is still up and about? Do I go now while we would be able to share quality time together? I had Sheila ask Ed. It was his call. His decision was for me to come now, as soon as possible. That was all I needed. I booked a flight, took three days off work, and off I went. It really was a good visit. We had deep spiritual conversations. I watched as he listened to judge shows on TV. It went by all too fast and then I was on my way home. It was the last time I would see Ed alive. Within two weeks, Ed quickly declined and went to be with the Lord. My friend and mentor for more than five decades had passed from death to life on August 7, 2011. It was four days before his seventieth birthday. I miss him.

Chapter 11

Hearing from the Lord

In the cry of Ed's heart, he challenged us not to waste time. Have you had those times of looking right into the face of your own mortality? For me and Ed, it was life-changing. Because of this reflection on my own mortality, I think differently about life now. Time is not guaranteed to us here on this earth. It's our human nature to think that we will live forever—or at least until we are one hundred years old.

It is a normal day for me when I am talking with the Lord all day long. Then, after each of my heart attacks, I had thirteen weeks off work for recuperation. I spent many hours in prayer. I now know how fragile life is, and I am compelled to make a difference in the hands of God.

What a difference God's tool has made. The lines of communication are forged when we spend time in prayer. Odd, isn't it? We live in the natural world. God lives in the supernatural world and the line of communication that bridges them both and connects us together is prayer!

In the beginning of this book, I made reference to my second heart attack. For a few minutes, when my heart stopped, I was dead in the body but alive in the spirit. Let me tell you that my conscious thoughts never stopped for one second. I was fully aware of myself. One second I was in an ambulance, feeling pain beyond my ability to tolerate, and the next instant I was above the ambulance.

February 6, 2006, was a very cold winter's day for us. It was snowing and there were six inches of it already on the ground. My wife, Mary, made the 911 call. It was near 6:30 p.m., and I got another answer to prayer. I had always wondered how we ended up living here, in this house, in this particular location. We knew that the people who had lived there before us moved because the man had a heart attack and died (how ironic). Don't get me wrong. I like the house and it is close to both our jobs. But I always envisioned myself living on a wooded lot somewhere. Why did God bring us to this home? Well, I know why now. It was three minutes from the firehouse—and an ambulance!

First the police arrived and immediately started to shovel the driveway so the gurney wouldn't have to roll in the snow. Others moved the kitchen set aside so they could roll me out of the house. Mary and I were in the computer room when this whole thing started. I thought I would go down to the kitchen when Mary went to answer the door. It would be easier for the medics to work on me if I was at the kitchen table. I didn't make it. I couldn't get past the hallway stairs. I lay back in the hallway, a prophetic symbol of transition, and two men started an IV in both arms. They gave me digitalis medicine for the heart, and they picked me up and placed me on a gurney. I had been here before. With my first heart attack, I knew there was nothing to worry about; I had seen my future. I would go on. However, this time, months in advance the Lord showed me that I would need immediate care and not to waste time in getting it. There I was, with a flurry of activity around me. As they rolled me out of the kitchen, Mary stepped up to me and said, "I love you, Tom." She was choking back the sobs. I didn't think to respond, I thought everything would work out as before. Not so!

In an Instant

You hear people say in fun, "I saw the light!" Sometimes they mean that they saw the spiritual realm split open. They were hanging in the balance between life and death. They say the light of heaven emanates in rays of brilliant light. While I was in the ambulance, freezing cold, it didn't matter. With all the tubes and wires, I lay there with no shirt or blanket on. The temperature was eight degrees, with heavy snow, and I was looking for the light! Quietly I asked the Lord, "Is this it?" I live near a golf course. We would have to travel along two sides of this golf course on our way to the hospital. It was on the second side of the golf course when it happened. Instantly, I noticed I was above the ambulance in the horizontal position, like I was in the ambulance. However, it was very peaceful for me while I was looking at the golf course. I felt no pain. Not for one second did my thoughts and mind stop working. I had constant awareness of my being, whether in the body or out of it. I then heard the voice of God speak to me. He said, "It is only while you are on earth that you can work for Jesus." The tone of the voice was masculine, as in the biblical description "deep like many waters."

I thought that a flurry of activity had taken place back at the house. Well, it was frantic in the ambulance below. They stopped the ambulance from moving when my heart flat-lined. With the defibrillator, they shocked my heart into working again. I have not told many people that when I got back into the ambulance and back into my body, I felt the power of God enter my chest. It was a stream of power an inch and half in diameter going deep into my chest, arching, and returning out again. It felt like it flowed in the shape of a horseshoe. This lasted almost a minute. I have felt the power of the Holy Spirit before and knew something supernatural was taking place. It was not the aftereffects of the defibrillator! He was healing the damaged portion of my heart, enough for me to stay alive until I reached the hospital.

What is the moral of the story? God works on principles! He has created doctors, nurses, medical equipment, and numerous medicines to bring healing. I had very bad side effects to the heart medicines that they wanted me to take after my first heart attack. So I didn't take them. Nor did I pursue alternate medications to keep my cholesterol low. I was destined for a second heart attack, and when it drew near, the Lord prepared me for it. I have thought long and hard about the precise words He said to me. I was not taking care of myself, and it would have shortened my life and marriage if God had not intervened. How stupid is that? I have gone through twenty years of intense growth, storms, and trials so that I could be used of God. I came close to throwing it all away. Hey, not that I didn't want to go to heaven. But the best is yet to come, and I want to stay around and work for Jesus!

Humbled by my experience, I sought God as never before. I had thirteen weeks off before I went back to work. I spent a lot of that time with the Lord. I had died! I didn't realize it until a doctor walked into my intensive care room and asked me how it felt to come back from the dead. Like the cancer of my brother-in-law, Ed, my type of heart attack only has a five percent survival rate. It is called the "widow maker." The artery closes up and blocks the flow of blood to the heart muscles. After hearing what the doctor said, all the pieces fell into place concerning what had happened to me. While I was at home, looking into the face of my own mortality, I sought Him as never before. I want to be used by God!

Prayer Changes Things

I tend to jump around a little, adding pieces of information, to draw you a word picture to grasp ahold of. So, let's take another jump. Men, it is part of our DNA to leave a legacy behind for our children and grandchildren to inherit. This is to help them know who we are as a family and where we have come from. As Christian men, we long to additionally leave a spiritual legacy in motion for our loved ones to live in the blessings of God. We set the course for their lives. Living our lives by God's principles, laws, and decrees, we steer a bloodline into the main channel of the river of God's provision.

In Chapter 4, I shared with you the gained knowledge of my family's generational cycles due to the sins of those who came before us. At this point in my life, I have stood in the gap for my children and extended family. I have watched the Lord turn those ungodly dynamics around to a positive position in the upward blessings scale.

I would like to tell you about a man named Palmer. I first met him, indirectly, when my wife and I sat down in the row behind him and his wife at church. We were new in the church and hardly knew anyone yet. It was odd how I disliked him instantly. Palmer was a man of multiple generations of Christians, and I could feel the blessings flowing in his life. They were flowing to his wife, children, and all those that he reached out to. This man lived the first commandment of God.

"You shall have no other gods before me. You shall not make for yourself an image in the form of anything in heaven above or on the earth beneath or in the waters below. You shall not bow down to them or worship them; for I, the Lord your God, am a jealous God, punishing the children for the sin of the parents to the third and fourth generation of those who hate me, but showing love to a thousand generations of those who love me and keep my commandments" (Exodus 20:3–6).

Clearly Palmer's forefathers had lived by this commandment, and he was receiving the fulfillment of God's love! His life was so different from my upbringing that it was like sandpaper rubbing over a patch of my skin. He irritated me, and at the same time I wondered what my life would have been like if we had flowed in the blessings of God as his family did. When I became born again, I was at level negative four on my Debris Scale. This man was at least seven levels above my life at a positive three. I felt it, can you tell? I could dwell longer on this with many more points to bring out on how Palmer challenged my life, but not at this point in the story.

Because I have loved Jesus with all my heart and I have been willing to follow Him no matter where He would bring me, He began His restoration in me. I would stand in the gap, and God would change our family line. That is why I consider John 10:10 to be my life's verse:

The thief comes only to steal and kill and destroy; I have come that they may have life, and have it to the full (John 10:10).

I have watched the Lord introduce issues and place them on my path of life to walk through. He would orchestrate a new result to my deeply dysfunctional life to the healthiness of Jesus Christ. The lost building-blocks of character in my childhood were reintroduced by His loving hands. Storm by storm, trial by trial, He rebuilt the parts of my life that the thief had destroyed, and He was transforming it into a lineage of blessings to all who follow after me. His spiritual legacy had come into my family.

God's Additional Plans

What do we leave behind on earth when we enter eternal life? I became obsessed with the spiritual decay of our culture and what condition it would be in for our children. The further we move away from God as a nation, the more our freedom and our liberty are lost. Restrictions on sharing the Christian faith with others are rapidly eroding away. Our culture is placing a Berlin wall around the hearts and souls of our children. It troubled me, and I would spend many hours in prayer asking the Lord to release grace to change this dynamic. In the vision I will share in a future chapter, He showed me that "the Lord has a plan."

I have wanted to bring this up for some time, and maybe it will fit in here. The prayers of intercessory prayer groups anywhere in the United States as well as my personal petitions are heard by God. They set into motion new adventures for me to enjoy. On several occasions, I watched how the Lord brought the two of us together. In one such occasion, I had a seven-part dream of a group consisting of the pastor's wife and five ladies. I saw them standing in prayer, humbling themselves before God, pleading with Him for the help only He could bring. It took several months for me to find them and for the provisions to fall into place. It is upon millions of Christian's hearts to see, and outpourings of God happen in our day. God's children are longing to see the supernatural realization of heaven and earth manifested in churches across America.

However, I am getting ahead of myself here. Let me introduce you to the third person God would bring me to meet through the Open Heaven website. The stage was being set for God's vessels to begin to bring a transfer of the spiritual ownership of the land! Let me make this point again. When church prayer groups enter into intercession and it reaches the heart of God, He releases and at times sends His servant to usher in change. If you have a prayer group, that is wonderful. If not, consider it for your church.

I want to be very serious for a moment. Prayer groups are a vital resource in achieving a breakthrough in the spiritual realm. But prayer groups that pray prayers outside of the boundaries of Scripture can open the doors to more harm than the godly good they are praying for. A must-read resource of any prayer group is the book, *Needless Causalities of War.*[1]

God brought me to Terrell, Texas. This is the location of the prayer group and the revelation of that seven-part dream.

Chapter 12

It's Time To Begin

In God's timing, the Holy Spirit guided me to do a search in the prophetic website (openheaven.com) on the title "Revival in Texas." I had entered this query in the search box and pressed the enter key. A church popped up in the little town of Corrigan, Texas. My first appointment from God through this prophetic website had been with Pastor Pat and his wife, Sue. My second God-ordained appointment from the website was getting acquainted with Pastor Phil. This relationship would further expand the vision (which I will share about in detail in a later chapter) to the churches in our entire region, not just one church in one city. The Holy Spirit is moving over the entire region, seeking those churches that will welcome a new move of God.

As you can imagine, the road to contacting Pastor Phil about revival in Texas was very compelling. Taking a risk that I might look foolish (this is becoming routine in my life), I sent off an inquiring e-mail. The article I found on the site search was filled with references of revival meetings by Pastor Phil. These revival services were being held in small Texas towns where miracles and healings were taking place. I had to know more about this godly activity taking place in the southern region of the United States.

I don't want to get too far ahead of myself at this point in the book. Relationships take time to build. In time this new acquaintanceship was predestined to become a deep friendship. I would correspond with Pastor Phil for nearly a year, and then it would be time for us to meet and begin to co-labor together. At this point, I didn't have a clue, but God knew the plan. In this initial e-mail, I shared with him the vision I had seen concerning central and east Texas.

Pastor Phil's return e-mail affirmed my information. (Whew!) He felt as if God was conveying to him and his church that they were moving in the right direction in their ministry. Pastor Phil was encouraged when he heard the geographic details of the vision. His church was right in the center of that area. He decided to read the e-mail to his congregation during a Wednesday night service. My e-mail was one of many confirmations that they received. Revival (a move of the presence of God) requires unity in a congregation. As the heart of a pastor leads his flock, others enter into his vision for the church. Taking time to seek God with fasting, prayer, and humility before the Lord is the recipe for the presence to come (see 2 Chronicles 7:14). This little church in Corrigan, Texas, became an intersection of heaven and earth, and touched lives in the surrounding communities. This would go far beyond the walls of their church to touch many nations.

Pastor Phil had been a pastor for nearly twenty-five years when I contacted him. For a few years, deep in his heart he felt an urging. The urging said, There must be more to be found in a relationship with God and we need to have it!

Ask and it will be given to you; seek and you will find; knock and the door will be opened to you. For everyone who asks receives; the one who seeks finds; and to the one who knocks, the door will be opened (Matthew 7:7–8).

Pastor Phil's desire for more caused him to ask questions. With his new information that there was a place where people could experience the presence of God, he pondered whether to take any actions to follow through. When he answered yes to that question, a new adventure began, including the start of many trips to Brownsville, Florida. Pastor Phil went to Brownsville to attend the revival meetings held at Pastor John Kilpatrick's church. He wanted to see firsthand what was happening there and to witness whether God was really in their midst.

I remember Pastor Phil telling me of the first trip he and several members of his church made together. They were riding in a borrowed passenger van from the business located next to his church. The group set off on a journey covering five hundred miles, traveling from Corrigan, Texas, to Brownsville, Florida. Their thirst for the living waters of God drove them on. They took the risk to venture outside the normal routine of their church life. They were not sure of what lay ahead. However, they were willing to take the chance to find out. Was it going to be a new beginning for Corrigan, Texas? Or would they find out that what was happening in the Brownsville church wasn't for them? I have come to know several pastors, and they are a breed of their own. I don't say that critically. I just didn't understand what leadership and ministry is like for them. There are many pressures involved in this dynamic.

Of utmost importance is the call of God: the empowering of the Holy Spirit to uphold them and hearing from the Lord daily for guidance and equipping. Was God calling Pastor Phil to a new spiritual walk? He had the hunger for more but were the stories he was hearing of the healings and signs really coming from the God he knew? Having that inner drive is one thing but being vulnerable as a pastor to seek out a new thing is another.

Pastors must be steadfast and solid in their faith and beliefs. They just can't preach it; they have to live it. Their personal lives and families are the models for others. I know a pastor who had the drive to start a new kind of church ministry to become seekers of all the prodigal sons and daughters in their community. The first phase of this plan was a larger building with expansion capabilities built into the plans. His current church had three hundred members. When he brought this new vision before the board, it came to a split vote. A slim majority sided with the pastor, and today that same pastor speaks to five thousand people a weekend, and five thousand hits on the church service are viewed on the church's website. Taking chances will bring change, and a pastor must be convinced he is being led by God and hearing His voice clearly.

How can a pastor lead if he has doubts himself? He must be a man of convictions and rooted strongly in the Scriptures. He must stand upon his denomination's mission statements, doctrines, and theologies. At a pivotal point in his life, Pastor Phil stood outside the front doors of the Brownsville church. Running through his mind was the question, *Am I hearing You correctly, Lord? Are You leading me here and now?*

Brownsville

In Brownsville, people would get in line out in front of the church hours before the doors opened. This was the only way that they could make sure they obtained a seat. A crowd had already gathered by the time Pastor Phil arrived with his group. People were coming for the nightly revival service, driven by their desire to be in the presence of God. Some had traveled hundreds or thousands of miles to be there. In this day's crowd, there were people not only from the local community but from all over the globe. Pastor Phil told me he was feeling nervous and had twinges of trepidation, wondering if the service was truly of God! Or was it comprised of ungodly events conjured up by fleshly emotions directing people down the wrong path, ultimately hurting them with bad religion? Despite his gut feeling to leave and head home without attending the service, they all walked through the doors together. They were ushered into a new move of God. Their time spent in the Brownsville revival meetings changed their lives.

I have a phrase I use from time to time—"ride the wave." Pastor Phil was in Brownsville to catch the new move of God happening there. He wanted to bring it back to his own church and community. You could bet that sooner or later traveling to Brownsville would become a chore. As they were attending the revival meeting, they felt the atmosphere rich in the Holy Spirit, and they liked it. Pastor Phil had become convinced that what was happening there was truly of God. When the winds and activity of the Holy Spirit moves, it can seem chaotic. It was their experiences and the fruit of the Holy Spirit that brought surety.

Back on his home ground, Pastor Phil sought the Lord earnestly for the revival to come to Corrigan, Texas. I love it when God shows up in power and glory, and that is exactly what happened. The power and glory of God came to Corrigan and started a new wave of healings and miracles for those in the community. For twenty-two weeks the church held revival meetings. A second wave of the Holy Spirit went for two years, touching countless lives.

Presence of the Holy Spirit

How did the presence of the Holy Spirit get to Corrigan? I have thought about the transition and have asked myself, How does it work? This is a spiritual exchange I want to understand. Our human nature is built up of many mind-sets and positions of faith. Our learned experiences in God leave us to form opinions on how all of this works. Human understandings don't often line up with God's ways. How do we gain a breakthrough to a new spiritual pathway? We lay our hearts before God leaning on Him to bring us to it!

My wife cooked me an awesome meal last night. Pot roast! It is one of my favorites. All the ingredients were in the house already. She got the carrots from the fridge and the potatoes from the cabinet. She could have skipped the green beans as far as I'm concerned. First, she pan-fried the pot roast before placing all of the items together in an 8 x 12 pan headed for the oven. Oh, don't forget that tasty gravy she whipped up. What's my point—other than that I enjoyed her meal?

God takes all the ingredients in our hearts and places them on the cutting board on the counter. He takes the faith and trims it up nicely with belief. He rearranges our mind-sets and points them to His new pathways. He cuts away falsehoods and introduces His spices of scriptural truth. Then the gravy is stirred together with the desires of our hearts to please Him. We deeply thirst to have more. Now is the time to scoop up all of the ingredients and place them in a pan destined for the oven. In the heat, all things come together and something new emerges.

That is a long way around to say that a pastor's seeking heart must find its own way to the breakthrough. God will take the ingredients of his life and turn the heat up. Whether it is caused by hardships, illness, loss, storms, or trials, the outcome of the journey will be a relationship. It is the relationship that now joins the Holy Spirit of God with the advent of the signs, wonders, and miracles. Once you have seen how much is available in our Christian walk, it is hard to settle for less.

I think an explanation of manifestations would be good here. It is miraculous when the Holy Spirit enters a place. The church became an intersection between heaven and earth. The love of God was so wonderfully rich it permeated the atmosphere within the building. It is moments like this when I am compelled to raise my hands upward. It is as if I am reaching out to my Father for Him to reach down and pick me up. This is just like a father and child who desire to be face-to-face and close to each other. In the moment, I understood what it meant to say "Abba!" I called out from my heart, my arms were stretched high, and I was filled with longing to be closer to Him. My soul was being satisfied by being in His presence.

In the Scriptures, one reference to the Holy Spirit's movements is "as the winds blow." In the atmosphere that I have described, you can see the movements by looking around. You can see those people who are being touched by the Lord. Other people are not impacted at all. I like the biblical story of the woman with the issue of blood (Luke 8:44). Jesus felt the power leave Him and the woman felt power enter her. She knew that she had been healed. Our God can create something from nothing. Creating new human parts isn't hard for Him to do. The woman had received her healing and the crowd around her didn't have a clue. As the wind blows.

In revival meetings, healings do take place. At times people will feel the Holy Spirit come upon them. They will feel the power enter their body and stream to the affected body part. Within seconds new tissue is made. Whatever was damaged is now made right. Other people are instantly healed without feeling the manifestation. Often those healed will be overwhelmed with an emotional response. Of course, there are some people who are not in the flow and wonder what is going on.

A great book to read is *Signs and Wonders*.[1] It clearly demonstrates the glory of God during revival meetings. I will make several references to this book of the life and ministry of Maria Woodworth Etter. It is a diary of her meetings and a step-by-step account of the miracles that happened to those whom she ministered to. When God invades a church, anything can and does happen. He touches His children as He wills. Visions may occur. A revelation of His holiness often takes place, changing a person forever. The baptism of the Holy Spirit is a common event where a person will speak in tongues. So great is the spiritually rich atmosphere, anything can take place.

Getting back to my correspondence with Pastor Phil, it was my hope that our paths would cross because I really wanted to meet him. Texas was a little too far for me to go for one service. Then I noticed on his website itinerary that he was going to be holding revival services at the Four Square Church in Lincoln, Nebraska. Lincoln is only a seven-hour drive from my home. I would be going right past America's largest truck stop just inside Iowa on Interstate 80. I love experiencing touristy places. I can feel it in the air—adventure! I was getting excited now—what had started as a vision from God was now bringing me to meet new people and new places. (For more information, Pastor Phil's website is Runningwithyoursecondwind.com)

Chapter 13

Unexpected Information

For forty-five years I have been working full time. In the early years, I was building a life with my first wife and raising our children. I loved being a dad. Life in the elevator trade is really more than a full-time job. It was hard on the family. The telephone would ring at all hours, and I would be off to work. Looking back, I remember taking off six weeks of vacation one year. However, I had accumulated twelve weeks of work time in overtime. It was part of the job, and I know many mechanics whose wives didn't like the constant interruptions it brought to family life. Despite all the interruptions the job would bring, we did have a lot of fun; it's in my nature.

I was driving down the road heading to Lincoln, Nebraska, to attend a set of revival services held by Pastor Phil. I had never met him in person. In the first several hours of driving down Interstate 80, I felt freedom and joy. There was no pressure of the job; no expectations to meet; no accountability owed to my customers or employer. It was only fun that lay ahead. It is rare for me to feel the elation in being on my own, even if it is for only a few days. I have only driven the I-80 corridor through Iowa and Nebraska once. We were coming home from a vacation. I remembered it as flat and straight, the most boring drive of my life. This day, Iowa was not what I remembered. I was looking at rolling hills and a gentle curving road. Could it have been the frame of mind that I was in the last time I was on this stretch of road? I was returning home after a vacation, one of those driving vacations that totaled over five thousand miles from start to finish. Now I remember.

I like to learn new things. Being an experiential type of person, I have a heightened sense of my spiritual feelings and emotions. I fed on what God was revealing to me about this place and now I am trying to put it into words for you. When traveling, I always have a plan. I checked into my hotel, got out my MapQuest pages, and drove around the city of Lincoln. Knowing where I am going is important. I never leave it to the last minute. So, locating the Foursquare Church where the meetings were to be held is on my list of things to do after I was settled in. Arriving early, I spent time walking around the church in prayer. I was noticing my nervousness as I was about to meet with Pastor Joshua and Pastor Phil. Oh boy, adventure three is about to begin.

The Foursquare Church was built to hold about one hundred people when full. The founder of the Foursquare Church was Aimee Semple McPherson who was a mighty woman of God. She was one of the great evangelists who impacted America with her faith in Jesus Christ. Here in Lincoln, a state capital and prominent college town, Pastor Joshua had invited Pastor Phil to come and share his relationship with the Holy Spirit with his people. Lincoln had become a spiritually dry place, but revival was in the air.

Things were starting to excel in my spiritual walk and journey. I was starting to learn about the social circles of pastors. Pastors enjoy word-of-mouth networking. At times there is an unspoken rule. (I need a lesson on that!) How do pastors get an invitation to speak? It is a hard road trip for a pastor to do his own cold-calling for speaking engagements. And many preachers consider self-promotion the kiss of death. A pastor must know a potential speaker/preacher or know someone who does know him. With some kind of reference, he will then determine if he would allow this person to influence his membership. It is a wise course of action to take. Concerning Lincoln, I was seeing things in the spiritual realm. I had received dreams as a message from the Lord for people whom I don't know. I found myself seeking out the people I was to meet and minister to. This goes against that unspoken rule, and at times closes the door. But my job is to follow the Lord and trust Him for the outcome that He has planned. In meeting the pastors on this trip, I felt like I was enrolled in the course "Understanding Pastors 101."

First Dream

The second class I would take in this college town was seeing what was happening in the spiritual realm there! On the first night, I had a dream. In this dream I was in the Foursquare Church with a very large stained-glass window. The sunlight was streaming through the window. I could clearly see the golden color of the stained-glass window rising from the floor to the ceiling. Suddenly, an invisible set of hands picked me up from behind, grabbing me under my armpits, and it began to lift me up toward the attic access panel. Feeling this spiritual presence, being lifted up and under the control of the Holy Spirit, I was very nervous. However, I have come to learn that if I can get into the attic I will see what is spiritually going on in this church. I will discover if it is godly or evil. In the attic, I will see the spiritual dynamic and the spiritual atmosphere for good or for bad. If I can get this information, it will be a major clue to determine what will be needed to move forward. In acts of repentance and the pleading for the forgiveness of sins, grounds to evil are removed and a transfer of spiritual ownership takes place. Reaching the attic, in this type of dream, helps me get acquainted with what negative grounds are being used to hold this church back. Slowly, I am being lifted up higher. Abruptly I stop and descend to the floor again. "No, wait!" I need to see what is happening in this church. If I don't make it to the attic, I will not get the information needed. I estimated that the Holy Spirit lifted me up halfway before lowering me back to the floor.

Next, I was in the physical plant side of the operations of the church. Again, I am lifted up by the Holy Spirit and toward the attic panel. To my shock, the same thing happens again. I obtain only half the distance I must go to open the attic panel and gain revelation, but I am returned to the floor. Once on the floor, there is the pastor and I begin to talk with him. From behind me, in the open door to the sanctuary, a man materializes wearing a Civil War uniform. A second soldier appears, and then a third. I get so disturbed that I wake up from my dream. Lying in my hotel room, I spend time committing all the details to memory. In the morning, I had a breakfast appointment with the pastors at Cracker Barrel. It should prove to be interesting!

For the sake of brevity, let me tell you the information I learned from the dream. First, Pastor Joshua was in a battle, a civil war with the people in the church. Pastor Joshua wanted to bring in the "new move of God." Because of his purity of heart before the Lord, he was being shown they could receive more. However, the church was stuck in the old wave of God that Aimee Semple McPherson had brought to the Foursquare Church. The young pastor and his family had poured all of their lives into bringing the "new move of God" to the church and the town of Lincoln. It took a heavy toll. A year after the revival meetings, Pastor Joshua left the ministry to work in the private sector so that he could earn higher wages to support his young, growing family. The congregation's constant opposition stopped Pastor Joshua's breakthrough, and it fell short. The demonic grounds stayed intact, and the spiritual life that was to come didn't happen on Pastor Joshua's watch, not because of lack of trying. He honored God in his service to the people.

Second Dream

The following night, I had another dream. I love the creativity in my godly dreams. At times, I can see in multidimensional pictures. In this dream I could see from inside of the church that there was water surrounding the foundation of the building. The water was six inches deep and crystal clear. Living water was now surrounding the church and extended out to the parking lot, and it was beginning to flow toward the community. This dream was a confirmation of God's response to the revival services. He was releasing His living water into a dry and spiritually lifeless community, bringing His life to them.

Third Dream

On Saturday night I had a third dream. In this dream I saw myself in my car beginning my drive home. I was driving through the side streets on the east side of the Foursquare Church. The living water was now three feet deep. As I drove toward the interstate, the crystal-clear, life-giving water from God was now rushing over the hood of the car. Crazy as dreams can seem, in my mind, I was wondering why the engine didn't die, being submerged in water that deep. As I continued to drive forward, the water flowed up the hood of the car and onto the windshield, making it necessary to turn on the wiper blades.

Divine Authority

I am touching on a point that came up during breakfast at Cracker Barrel. Pastors are usually concerned about having intercessors and prophetic people around. I have learned in my walk with the Lord that there is a divine order of authority in the body of Christ. Pastors are the people responsible before the Lord and held accountable by Him for what happens in their churches. I understand that if you are responsible you have the last word and the ultimate say in what goes on in your church. I shared that understanding with Pastor Joshua and Pastor Phil, and I was surprised to hear their sigh of relief. Too many times they had experienced a rogue minister or intercessor bringing disunity and a message that didn't line up with the plan they held for their church members. I am glad I verbalized my position; it helped relax the atmosphere. I didn't know these men had had more than enough bad experiences to warrant caution.

Meeting Pastor Phil was the highlight of the trip. He was a man who loves people like God loves them. I could see the hand of God upon his life and ministry. Signs and wonders followed his meetings and he ushered in the presence of God, which impacted those people in attendance. One lady who received prayer went under the power of the Holy Spirit and for thirty minutes lay on the sanctuary floor. She experienced an open vision of heaven. Her life has been forever changed by this glorious experience. She wasn't looking for this to happen; it was God's gift to her.

What Did I Learn?

One of the questions I often ask the Lord is "Why?" Why was Lincoln, Nebraska, a spiritually dry place? Why were the pastor and the congregation engaged in a civil war concerning the spiritual direction of their church? Why did the living water released in the revival service grow daily?

One night in a dream the Lord showed me about living water. I saw myself living in a creek ravine. There were rock ledges and steep walls lining the creek bed. I had my spot in the creek; it was mine and that is where I stayed. Others lived along the creek and had their claim to an area they owned. It was a community. We had spiritual life and thrived in the creek of living water—until the water level began to decline. Day after day the amount of water dwindled, and the community became very concerned. Then it happened: the living water stopped flowing, and all the blessings that were in the water ended too. We braced for the darkness to arrive. Right on the heels of no living water arrived evil and its minions. Our spot along the creek now lay void of the presence of God and all His blessings, including protection from the enemy. We were all on our own. This is something that is now happening in the United States.

Now I make the comparison of the dream to the community surrounding the church. The community was dry, void of living water, and occult activities arrived. In Lincoln, in the vacuum of no living water, the prevalent spirit was that of humanism. The works of the spiritual life in the Holy Spirit are unique. When it is alive, it is thriving and vibrant. When it is dry, it is lifeless and powerless.

Imagine a beautiful, live floral arrangement growing in rich, fertile soil. This represents the spiritual life found in the Holy Spirit. When the presence of the Holy Spirit is gone, those same flowers become like a silk plant; they look very much the same, but there is no spiritual life in them.

On a personal note, this trip brought a new discovery for me. The Lord showed me information through dreams and visions about the pastor and church that I was about to interact with. This was new for me. It was still difficult to attach the right person to the corresponding dream—baby steps—I'm still learning! When I left Lincoln, the messages for this area stopped, and I was looking forward to the next adventure.

Chapter 14

Preparation for the Conference

"On call" is my status when it comes to my relationship with the Holy Spirit. Or maybe I could say my status is "I'm available." This is the part of the journey that I like—being spontaneous. I never know when the Lord is going to give me a dream or vision download. So let me build a bridge into the summer of 2009, several months before the pastor's conference in Gonzales, Texas. My wife and I were on vacation in Estes Park, Colorado. What a beautiful mountain town it is, at the doorstep to the Rocky Mountains National Park and all of its grandeur. Ice-cold water in the mountain streams ran throughout the town. One of those streams ran past the foot of our lodge. Not more than ten feet away, in its swift pace rushing on by, we listened to the song it was serenading us with.

Why is it that the sound of water has a calming effect upon our spirits? My inward reflections stirred as I watched and listened to the waters pass. Its hypnotic, crystal-clear flow hides no content in its bed. I was curious, though, to know how it stays within its banks. I heard it say in its babbling voice, "Can't hold me back. I'm rushing to destiny's shore." For this young stream, its path is set, resting on the eastern side. From mountains high to valleys low, the Great Divide determines that this young stream will never see our western side. No, it will flow to places that grow and nourish those who reside there. As the stream flowed into the fertile ground of the great plains so too does the living water flow to our fertile hearts and bring new growth and life to us.

Sunday Church on the Road

When traveling, come Sunday we always look for a church to visit, and in Estes Park there was a church nearby. With the help of a visitors' guide, including a map of the town, we were able to locate the address and building. It was a small church with about twenty-five people in the service; as is often the case, the people were very welcoming to visitors. The senior pastor wasn't preaching this day; the associate pastor gave the sermon. It wasn't the message I remember; it was the spiritual atmosphere that got my attention. I thought, *They are poised for the heavens to open!* I got excited about what I was seeing and the potential for a being part of a new move of God. To me, they were very close to a breakthrough in the spiritual realm.

After the service, we patiently waited until I could speak with the senior pastor and share with him what I was seeing. He was totally open to the things I said and agreed that the Lord was taking them down a road toward an open heaven above their church. The realization of his desire for more of God would impact the area with wonderful blessings. We talked about the territorial spirits hindering the region, and I mentioned Pastor Phil and his revival ministry. I don't know about you, but I always wonder what part I am to play in divine appointments. However it turns out, we enjoyed the service, and I was delighted to see the stirring of the Holy Spirit in this town.

Intersection

Did you ever hear someone say, "Oh, by the way"? I will use this phrase to introduce another line of thinking leading into a rabbit trail in hopes of bringing together several pieces of information for a complete thought. So, "Oh, by the way," let me share with you two Scriptures relating to when heaven and earth intersect.

As he (Paul) was approaching Damascus on this mission, a light from heaven suddenly shone down around him. He fell to the ground and heard a voice saying to him, "Saul! Saul! Why are you persecuting me?" (Acts 9:3–4 NLT)

Another verse to share is:

While Zechariah was in the sanctuary, an angel of the Lord appeared to him, standing to the right of the incense altar. Zechariah was shaken and overwhelmed with fear when he saw him (Luke 1:11–12 NLT).

Here is the rabbit trail. The spiritual experiences that I have through dreams or visions can often be disturbing. In our natural environment, we live in an organized world within boundaries. There is comfort in the natural world where we exist. The spiritual realm is entirely different, even though it is surrounding us at all times. When the two intersect at the same place at the same time, the comfortable boundaries are ushered aside and the spiritual atmosphere is manifested. I am not saying this feels bad, but it feels unnatural and that can be disconcerting.

I always struggle in explaining the experiences I have in the Lord. It is hard to help people see the spiritual message coming out of my encounter with Him. Let me say, in the beginning, when the spiritual atmosphere would shift and open, it happened almost always in the middle of the night while I was sleeping. Days before an event, the Lord always prepared me to yield to Him. After the encounter, I would spend a lot of time in prayer seeking the Lord to show me it was truly Him. I needed to know beyond a shadow of a doubt before I would want to continue. Who wouldn't want it validated with Scriptures and those in the faith who have gone before us? I grew in confidence and learned to walk by the Holy Spirit of God.

Sunday night, in our lodge alongside our mountain stream, nicely nestled up against a rocky cliff, I was called to intercede for this town. I can always sense the spiritual atmosphere begin to change. This night the Lord allowed me to encounter the spirit inhibiting the town's spiritual growth. I immediately started to pray for this place. Leaning on the Holy Spirit to reveal to me the issues where sin had created grounds and strongholds, I prayed for forgiveness of these sins. Two nights in a row this happened before we moved to our next vacation spot. Two nights in the spiritual realm I interceded for them. I left wondering what impact and change my intercession had brought to this community.

Next Assignment

It was some weeks later, after several conversations with Pastor Phil in hopes of arranging revival meetings in Estes Park, I had a dream. There were four parts in this dream: the first two showed me the pastors at the Estes Park church were going to reject Pastor Phil's offer to help with opening the area to signs and wonders. It was possible because Pastor Phil had a scheduled service in Greeley, Colorado, in three months' time. That meant he would be only thirty miles away. It was not meant to be; the door was closed. The third part of my four-part dream was Pastor Phil waiting with me until God's next appointment. The fourth segment showed me I was going to encounter a pastor in a place I didn't recognize, who would assign me work to do in his church, and I would have a spiritual confrontation with evil there. I saw the triumphant victory and knew the outcome in advance. In the near future, God would bring together the pastor's conference in Gonzales, Texas, and open the door for me to attend. This is where the fourth piece of the dream would come into reality.

Chapter 15

The Road to Gonzales

The driving distance between my home and Gonzales, Texas is 1,211 miles. It had never even occurred to me I would make this trip one day. The doorway into Texas was through my friendship with Pastor Phil. Unity in the Holy Spirit can bring two total strangers together and make it seem as if they had been friends for a lifetime. It was Pastor Phil who encouraged me to attend the pastor's conference being held in Gonzales, Texas, on November 18, 2009. I had shared with him the vision of their inheritance (the presence of God) coming to Texas and then flowing into the southern United States. It was after my wife and I talked and spent time in prayer that I accepted his invitation.

Visiting Family

Two things happened immediately. I have two nephews living in Texas whom I have never visited. I couldn't go to Texas to speak at a conference and not try to see both of them. Texas is the largest state in the lower forty-eight. What was I thinking? James lives near Dallas and Edward lives just south of Gonzales. I needed a driving plan. The second thing that crossed my mind was, *Is God going to use me to be an intercessor while I am in Texas driving from place to place?* I love those divine appointments. I would be looking for them beyond the obvious while I was connecting with family.

Deep in the Heart of Texas

What was my driving plan? I bought tickets from Midway Airport taking me to William P. Hobby Airport, in the south Houston area. The plan was to rent a car and leave Hobby heading north to Dallas up Interstate 45 to where James lived.

My visit with James and Sandy was filled with family memories and getting reacquainted. Now our evening was over, and I picked up my room key. I would soon find out if the Lord was going to use me for intercession in this town or for this region. It had been a long day, and sleep was on my mind.

Being an intercessor for a place or a region, as I mentioned in the previous chapter, often happens in the night. It is while I am dreaming that the Lord will show me issues to focus prayer on or I will have an encounter with a regional spirit with control of the area. I will pray on behalf of a city, town, county, and at times a state. So, as I was drifting off to sleep, I wondered what the night would hold. This night I had a sweet, restful night ushering in a new day with new adventures.

Off and Running

I had a deadline to meet! Sleeping in was not on the schedule. Anyone who knows me understands the phrase "packing it in!" On our family vacation I always have planned for events throughout the day. I usually plan too many things and I want to get in all I can on my trip to maximize my enjoyment. My poor kids would be drooping, dragging, complaining about being tired—and that was by noon! If there was something to experience or see of the natural wonders, we experienced it or saw it.

On this solo trip, I would travel sixteen hundred miles in just eight days, which isn't hard to do in Texas. In just a few hours I would rendezvous with Pastor Phil in San Antonio. The two of us would be staying there overnight before we would continue on to Gonzales. Pastor Phil loved San Antonio very much, and he sold me on the idea of seeing it while I was in Texas. I am glad that he did. He was my tour guide.

It was near Austin, Texas, that my phone began to ring. "Hello, Tom, how much farther do you have to go to reach San Antonio?" Pastor Phil asked. I told him that according to my GPS I had two hundred and forty-five miles to go to reach my hotel. His response was, "I have exactly two hundred and forty-five miles on my GPS to my hotel!" But he was coming from Corrigan, Texas. What an odd coincidence traveling the vast area of Texas down I-35. I have heard prophecies about revival coming to the I-35 corridor and now I was driving on this interstate.

Like my dad, I had my arm slung out the driver's side window, enjoying every minute of the new scenery, fresh air, and freedom. Rachel, my GPS voice, started talking to me about needing to turn. Already I was in San Antonio. Several quick turns and there was the hotel. Checked in, bags up in the room, now it is time to see the town and the river walk. In no time at all, waiting just outside the hotel, Pastor Phil drove up in his car and off we went.

San Antonio is a very beautiful city with its famous river walk. Right from the start, I was dazzled by the way it was all set up. There were concrete sidewalks raised above the waterway. Shops and restaurants were open to the view of the water and the tour boats were quietly passing by. The trees and shrubs adorned with lights twinkled in the night. The roads, set above, crisscrossed the river. It was a winding maze of overpasses and trails along the river, and I was definitely lost within a mile or so. Hotels with atrium lobbies opened up so the guests could take in the view. It would take time to explore the river walk, and I really wanted to see the Alamo before it closed for the day.

A Purpose for My Side Trips

An orchestra is a group of performers on various musical instruments. The "conductor" of an orchestra leads all the performers in the presentation of music. He brings harmony out of all the different instruments and through his expression guides each musician by bringing out their best. He does this not by rigid control, but by leadership and confidence in all their abilities to play and perform to his expectations.

While Pastor Phil and I were at the Alamo, absorbing the richness of history in the battles for Texas' freedom, I began to see the hand of God leading. He was leading His orchestra of performers in the battle for spiritual freedom for the souls of men. I would later learn why God had chosen Gonzales, Texas, for the pastor's conference. But for now, I clearly saw Pastor Phil's family history. "Sam Houston" played a part in the battle for Texas' freedom. Pastor Phil's grandmother was a "Houston." In his lineage are people who fought in the battle for Texas' independence. Now Pastor Phil was playing a part in the spiritual battle for the souls of Texans and beyond. The tour of the Alamo was very moving—a "proud to be an American" type of moving. How important it is for us to remember those who fought for our freedom! Knowing our history helps us to know who we are as a people and a nation.

How can you decide on a restaurant with so many wonderful choices? We returned to the river walk to have our evening meal. Our first choice, an upscale Italian cuisine, had an hour-long wait. We were too hungry for that. Several others places caught our interest, but we ended up at Joe's Crab Shack with a table right on the sidewalk where we could do the maximum people-watching. I wanted to be able to wave to the friendly faces on the tour boats passing by. Did you know that Joe's Crab Shack makes it a point to take pictures of patrons and post them on their website? I didn't. It was a pleasant surprise when I got home to print out our picture for a memory of that awesome evening. I got the overview tour, fitting in the most we could before we left in the morning. I can't wait to visit this wonderful city again. San Antonio is one of the best feel-good places I have ever visited. No wonder Pastor Phil wanted to return and show me around. It is a Texas must-see city!

Chapter 16

The First Day

"Come and Take It"
The battle cry in the Battle of Gonzales

The population of Gonzales, Texas, is 19,610; it comprises 5.1 square miles and was my destination for God's next divine appointment! We serve a great God, don't we? Every adventure has great depth to it, and all these wonderful clues and symbols lead us to His comprehensive works. I did not know the history of Gonzales, Texas, before my arrival. All I knew was that the door had opened up for me to speak and release the vision God had shown me on January, 20, 2006: Inheriting the Land!

It was Sunday morning and the first of four days of meetings was about to take place. Pastor Phil and I arrived in Gonzales early. We both had different plans for Sunday church. My brother-in-law, Ed (whom you met in an earlier chapter), was staying at his son Edward's home. Ed had towed his camper from Sarasota and set it up in front of his son's shed. That enabled the two of them to meet me for church with Pastor Glynn. Right on time, the three of us converged at the front door.

The church was a building of modest construction. Wooden pews, brown carpeted floors, florescent lighting, and wood paneling on each side wall. At the front of the church there was one raised step so that everyone could see the pastor when the message was being given.

Beyond the platform, along the back wall, was the baptistery. There were doors on either side leading up to the baptistery and another door leading to dry clothes. There were several offices on each side of the sanctuary, a cry room and hospitality room at the back. When the church would be full, it held one hundred and fifty people or so.

I hadn't seen my nephew Edward in more than ten years. He was now fortyish and had a face full of a beard. Warm hugs were given all around and quickly we entered the front door and took a spot near the back. I was in Texas for a church service and I didn't know what to expect. Deep in the heart of Texas and the country-and-western-style worship music filled the air. I liked it! During the service, as I often do when in a different church for the first time, I started to pray prayers of intercession. It was near the middle of the service. I had been there for about twenty minutes. I say that, because as soon as my mind began to pray, a strong, evil, repelling force began pushing back against my mind. The harder I tried to pray, the stronger the push back became. Immediately, I knew what was going on and stopped my prayers. The service was over, and I began thinking about the encounter.

A Look Back

Back in Chapter 14, I relayed the details of a four-part dream, the first three were completed, and this was where the fourth part of the dream came in. In this church, evil had grounds because of some sin, and it was actively counteracting the spiritual vitality that the pastor was trying to release. This church is the place where I was to confront evil, to fulfill the fourth part of the dream and be a victor in Jesus Christ.

I barely knew Pastor Glynn. We had only had about five conversations on the phone before the conference. How was he going to take it when I approached him with the information that a demon was in the church building? I knew beyond a shadow of doubt that I was supposed to be there. I knew beyond a shadow of doubt what the outcome would be. Now, how would I go about this matter of talking to him about it? For this to work, we would have to be in unity. He was the pastor and spiritual leader of this church. All things were to flow through him, and all authority was on his shoulders before God. Pastor Glynn had the ultimate say, and rightly so.

At the conclusion of the service, I asked Pastor Connie's advice on where we could eat Sunday brunch. She gave us several choices and said the "Cow Palace" (chuckle) was just down the street, only five minutes away. It was just the right suggestion because it was on Route 183 leading out of town. It was the road heading toward Edward's home. Off we went.

I love the uniqueness of different locales. Directly behind the restaurant was a large stockyard pen holding a group of cattle. "The food can't get much fresher than that!" Ed said as we walked in the front door of the restaurant. Inside it spoke volumes about a business in a holding pattern with its décor. I would say forty years of memories shared by the folks living in Gonzales echoed in this place. It remained unchanged and held deep roots to what the town is: "cattle country."

The familiar sight brought a sense of who they were and where they had come from in their lives. I need to say that all of the people that I met in Gonzales and in the other towns I have spoken of, Texans know who they are and their family histories. This strong sense of identity breeds confidence in their lives. They are determined, strong, and no-nonsense people. They strive on challenges and hard work. Pedigree plays a major role in claims to their history and accomplishments in the community and the state of Texas. In the Midwest, many families moved to the Chicago area because of jobs, and that is how both sides of my family lines came to the Chicago area. In Texas, however, generation after generation of Texans have stayed on the land owned by their families for years. In Chicago, we own lots; in Texas, they own acres! Okay, that was one of those "rabbit trails."

As the three of us walked into the "Cow Palace," we sat down in a booth on the south wall. Quickly we ordered when Pastor Phil popped in the door and came right over to meet my family. I was surprised to see him and I introduced him to my brother and his son. I was glad that he came.

Onward to Meet Edward's Family

After the meal, Pastor Phil and I were on different paths. The three of us were on our way to Edward's house and Pastor Phil had plans with his free time before that night's first service. While I was following those guys back to the house I had time to think about the spiritual warfare at Pastor Glynn's church. It is times like this when I go deep into thought, hoping to see all I can understand and gain knowledge for an intercession. I need the right words to use when I talk with Pastor Glynn. In those moments I lifted up prayers for God's timing to come into play. He had shown me six months ago this exchange/encounter was placed across my path for His will and His spiritual gain. I was just the vessel being used for it to happen and come together for His outcome. I saw the victory in the spiritual realm, and now I will see the victory in the natural realm. I would come to know that Pastor Glynn is a prayer warrior! In his many hours of pleading with God for the souls of men, God had a plan and soon it would start to flow. The timing had come.

In the late afternoon, I met up with Pastor Phil and we checked into the motel. We found the host church by 6 p.m. and participated in an hour of prayer before the meeting began. The host church had a sanctuary large enough to hold several hundred people.

As many as five local churches were contributing to the conference. My goal was to meet as many pastors as possible while I was there. I brought with me a gift book I wanted to give them. To me, *Signs and Wonders*[2] is a Holy Spirit manual of His manifestation during visitations of the Lord. I was expecting God to do great things in Gonzales and sharing this book would help the pastors and others validate a Holy Ghost revival and what happened to people when He shows up.

Pastor Johnny would be the worship leader for the conference. I had never met him before. However, he and Pastor Phil often traveled together holding revival meetings. Pastor Johnny not only was musically talented but also sang a pretty good tune. Not being accustomed to a Texan style of worship, I found this new expression of worship to be very uplifting. He played an acoustic guitar and I have always enjoyed the rich sound that comes from this instrument. The format was set: worship, message, worship, then open prayer for healing and beyond. The first set of worship songs were toe-tapping music. They were quick-paced and glorifying to God. The message revealed that God heals today and was followed by a call to come forward to receive prayer. I got so excited because we were on the edge of the spiritual realm opening up; I could feel it. I always love being in the fullness of the presence of God. In my spirit, I could tell we were poised to have a visitation from the Lord.

Where's the Spirit Moving?

I am a watcher! I want to see what God is doing, so I will look to see what manifestations are occurring to different people. Tonight, the front of the church is full of people spontaneously coming forward in hopes of God meeting their need. Some have physical needs and others need emotional healing. Some people long for a deeper walk in the Lord and any gift released to them is pure joy. Deliverance from strongholds and spiritual healings will also be realized by some tonight.

It just occurred to me that you might pose the question, "Tom, what is it like when the atmosphere opens and heaven and earth become an intersection?" Referring back to my spiritual sensitivity, I feel the atmosphere shift. At first it is like feeling power flowing over my body—not just the outside, but the inside as well. Having worked with electricity for most of my career, I have had a shock or two. In my younger life, a shock was no big deal. I would jump, yell out, shake it off, and move on. One day, while working on what we called "a balanced bridge detector," my boss and Jesse, my best friend, were helping me troubleshoot. That means I did all the work and they watched. This type of detector runs at 1,000 cycles a second, unlike the household power that is set at 60 cycles a second. Well, I got shocked by the balanced bridge detector in front of my boss and best friend. The power hit me so hard that my recoil sent me into the corner of the elevator cab in a heap, curled up in a ball. Stunned for sure, my two friends were laughing so hard that I thought my boss was going to have a heart attack right there. That experience brought them years of laughter and tears.

The power of the Holy Spirit has the same effect as in our earthly electricity without the pain associated with it. A light flow of power began to flow through me conveying to me the atmosphere was beginning to shift from closed to open. That's when I became excited.

That first night was the beginning of better things to come. People who had been diagnosed with various medical conditions received healings, and God restored their lives to normal. Often when illnesses come into our lives, whether it is physical, emotional, or spiritual, it impacts us. We wonder if our lives will ever return back to normal. Jesus died for our sins and He carried our illnesses too. Divine healing is still available today, and many in the meeting were stunned as they felt the power of the Holy Spirit enter their bodies and injured damaged body parts were restored to normal. This first meeting ended with a house filled with peace and joy. Often people linger on in the house of the Lord just because it feels good to be there.

The ladies of the church had a meal waiting for the participating pastors, and I was glad to be included. This one-on-one time brought a very rich exchange and allowed me to get to know them. We had about forty people for the post-meeting gathering. Just weeks before leaving for the conference, I had a dream showing me two people that I was to help. So when I met the two people assigned to help me, I had a different agenda due to my dream.

Pastor Jim is a shoot-from-the-hip, straightforward speaker. He doesn't have time to sugarcoat any message. It is the word of God, and he allows the double-edged sword to do its work with no apologies. I'm not saying that he is rough or rude—not at all. The power in his word impacts our comfort zones, the light of his word hit our souls, and we need to choose: do we listen or do we flee?

Pastor Jim is a cancer survivor. He had a rare form of cancer in his ear. He went through all the treatments and finally succumbed to surgery. His right ear had to be removed and all the skin surrounding it. In today's medicine and new options, the medical staff enlarged his stomach and removed a section of stomach skin as a substitute for the cancerous skin connected to his ear. The hard-riding motorcycle lover was humbled by his new appearance. It changed him, but for the stronger. He may be hard to look at in the beginning, but his personality and love for life and love for Jesus takes the front seat in his outlook. The man really is contagious for the Lord. Pastor Jim reminds me of the story where Jacob wrestled with an angel until he would bless him (see Genesis 32:26). In his illness, Pastor Jim wanted more of Jesus, more of the Holy Spirit in his life and ministry. I admire many of the pastors here at the conference for their hard work and desire to please Father God. The Lord had heard the cry of Pastor Jim and his wife, Anita. He has set before them a divine appointment!

Double Duty

It often happens to me that I have a godly dream with an assignment but no one to apply it to. Then a new adventure begins. Several weeks before I left for Gonzales, the Lord shared with me in a dream that two people were being ravaged by evil forces. It was hard to watch the man and woman who were being attacked, and they were without spiritual weapons to defend themselves. In addition, I was to be an agent of forgiveness for them, praying for the forgiveness of sins that the Holy Spirit would reveal to me at the time it would be needed. In that first meal after this first service, I had a very strong suspicion that it was Pastor Jim and Anita whom the Lord had prepared me to pray for. In the days ahead, I would look for confirmation and the opportunity to minister to them both. But for now I was adjusting to this new environment of pastors and clergy. It was a different life laid out with different guidelines that I would need to learn.

Being the host church, Pastor Lynn and his wife had their hands full with weeks of additional work added to the normal routine of church life. They were loving, warm, and kind. I believe it was in the heart of Pastor Lynn to see his community be impacted by enabling guest speakers to come and release their gifts into Gonzales and the surrounding community. It says in 2 Chronicles 7:14 that when God's children humble themselves and pray He will hear from heaven. I believe God heard the prayers and cries from all the intercessors and pastors who wanted more of God to come into their area. Meeting all the new people who are sincere servants of God impacted my life. I was honored to be among them.

Of all the pastors that I met at this conference, Pastor Lynn was the busiest, and that limited my time to get to know him. It was at that point that two things became clear to me! God had set in motion two divine appointments: Pastor Glynn's church and Pastor Jim and Anita's personal lives. Their stories would unfold rather quickly, but this was only the beginning of the things God had in store for me and the pastors whom I would meet at the conference.

Chapter 17

Day Two of the Conference

At the close of Sunday's meeting, a schedule was finalized for the agenda for the next couple of days. Over the course of the remaining three days, several locals were pinpointed for group prayer. During a group discussion, it was brought up that there were several places in town and nearby where occult activities and rituals took place. Placed on the discussion table was the question: "Do we actually go to these places for group prayer?" Several ideas were developed. In the morning, we would all meet at a local restaurant for breakfast and then leave for group prayer at the Gonzales Museum. Still pending was the suggested group prayer at the places of occult activities.

Again, my family expression was apropos: "We really pack it in." This trip was very much like being on vacation for me, so naturally I enjoyed a full day. Closing the door to my room at the end of the day, I was tired and quickly got ready for bed. I set the air-conditioner on low, turned off the lights, got into bed with the pillows just so, then fell asleep.

I am not an early riser. However, the next morning I woke up and sat straight up around 8 a.m. I need to talk with Pastor Phil. I had a message for him. During the night I had three dreams with the same message presented in three different ways. Throwing some clothes on, I headed to the coffee/breakfast room thinking I might find him there. He was already on his second cup of coffee. I sat down and began to tell him of the dreams and the message. The point was clear: "Don't go to the places where the occult activities occurred!" All three dreams were pertaining to lawyers in the legal arena. Two opposing parties were in dispute. Nothing was resolved and each dream ended in a stalemate. This was my first lesson in dealing with territorial strongholds. It was what I would call a "tit for tat exchange." My experience with this type of exchange is never profitable! If we went to the places where the rituals were held, we would lose the battle for ushering in the Kingdom of God at the pastor's conference meetings. I learned the dynamic for bringing change to a place/church/region is to focus on God alone. To worship Him, we must humble ourselves before Him and seek repentance. This is the beginning of understanding the formula in 2 Chronicles 7:14. In this dynamic, with this focus, in an atmosphere of repentance, Father God hears the cries of His children and sends angelic helpers and godly provisions. I repeat: He sends help from above to bring healing to the land! To engage evil in an attempt to free the region from demonic strongholds would bring an onslaught of trials, storms, and troubles. Let me refresh a directive here: If you are going to do intercession for your church/town/region, it is very important to read the book *Needless Casualties of War*[1] as a reminder of what to do and what not to do.

Pastor Phil was troubled by the idea of targeting prayer at the sites of occult practice as well. We agreed not to include those sites in the suggested places pinpointing prayer. It was nearing 9 a.m., time to meet the gang at the Mexican restaurant that we had previously selected. This was my first breakfast with a group of pastors, and it was a great time of fellowship. To see and talk with each pastor when they were not pastoring their church members and to have a chance to know them as regular folks was a treat!

Group Prayer

Within a mile of the restaurant was the Gonzales Museum. About nine of us gathered on the front steps before it opened for the day and held our prayer meeting. I remember the cold chill in the midmorning, even though our prayers were targeted and piping hot. We each took turns lifting up concerns to the Lord. We asked the Lord to forgive the corporate sins of the community, a vital element in breaking up evil's strongholds held against the town. I believe the spiritual realm was shaken that day. The beginning of new things to come in taking back the land took place that day (spiritually speaking, God would inhabit the land and transfer ownership to His people).

Plowing the Ground

Let me share with you an experience that I had several years ago. I was at a conference in Chesterfield, Missouri, billed as a "God Encounter." A meeting room was set up in a local hotel with a capacity of about one hundred people. Pastor Richard was one of the speakers scheduled for Saturday afternoon. We were in the praise and worship segment preceding his presentation. I was seated in the back of the room feeling the sweet presence of God, lost in the atmosphere of praise. Pastor Richard was standing, in the front, engulfed in worship himself. He is a man more than six feet tall and was directly in my view—hard to miss.

As I focused on him, I saw a vision about him. I saw a man, a huge man, standing on the face of the earth. In terms of measurement, he was twenty-five miles tall and positioned above the state of Florida. He was facing northwest. My view was from behind and up above him. From this perspective the curvature of the earth could be seen clearly, as well as the boundaries of the United States. I watched as he took several strides in a northwesterly direction and suddenly stopped over the state of Alabama. Both of his feet were firmly on the ground. I watched as he redistributed his weight with a bounce in his knees, sending pressure through his feet to the ground below. The effect on the ground was like watching the effect of dropping a pebble into a pond with a ripple emanating outward in a circular fashion. I saw three or four seismic waves flow through the ground like the waves of an earthquake. I continued to watch as he again began to walk northwest in direction. He stopped at another location of our country repeating the same dynamic.

This was a new lesson for me. The Lord was showing me that He had ministers who plowed the regions affecting the spiritual realm. This was the beginning of changing seasons. Pastor Richard understood the role he was playing, not only in the spiritual realm but also in the regions. He does one-on-one ministering at the conferences. A place, region, or state may have spiritual darkness and the lack of God's living water. But when prayer touches the heart of God, especially intercessory prayer, God sends provision. This lesson showed me the steps used in plowing the spiritual realm to the realization in the natural realm. It showed me the effect it has in harvesting the souls of men. Pastor Richard and his wife, Jodi, are contagious Christians. They usher in an open heaven to the body of Christ wherever they minister. They bring in revival.

Continued Prayer

Returning to the new move of God in Gonzales, this band of pastors gathered together to petition Father God to for a fresh awakening. We left the restaurant and drove directly over to the museum. We gathered on the steps to plead in unity to God for the region. I was there to release the vision of inheriting the land that I had seen years earlier. I will share this with you in a later chapter. Sheltered from the wind, we stood on the steps built with high side walls. It was a great windbreaker; we needed to stay warm. It was Pastor Glynn who took the lead and brought us through a time of intercession. We all had a time of prayer. Then he brought this gathering to a close. When it ended, I seized the opportunity to spend time with him. Quickly I asked him if I could tag along. He asked me if I was open to prayer at his church's property outside of town. I accepted his offer.

The drive took three minutes tops. There was no formal parking lot. Everyone just parked on the grass in front of the building. Before we exited the car, we talked for a few minutes, getting to know each other better. He was a brother in Christ and deeply committed to the Lord. We were two lives converging together for one purpose—to serve God.

While in the car, I realized this was the doorway I needed to bring up the experience I had had in the Sunday service. The grassy parking lot became the appointed time. To my surprise, as I told him about my encounter with an evil spirit, it didn't impact Pastor Glynn in the negative manner that I was expecting. Neither did he reject my notion of a demonic presence in the church. As a matter of fact, many people who were working in the church had often heard someone running within the building. It was eerie. They could not gain victory over this strange presence. Pastor Glynn had inherited this problem when he and Pastor Connie came to Gonzales. They had previously been in Alaska where he was a circuit preacher. Being a bush pilot, or a bush preacher, he traveled around by airplane.

We entered the back door of Pastor Glynn's church and began to anoint the building. When we reached the final three rooms, I could feel a chill in the air and sensed that evil was there. We began to pray for forgiveness of sins. The once troubled atmosphere within the church has now been replaced with the peace of God. The fourth part of my dream at Estes Park was now complete.

What Are the Chances?

Here is a sidebar from the chapter: I was there in Gonzales in November 2009. In September 2011, I joined a pastor Facebook group. When I became a member, I got to know the group administrator. This was his creation for pastors and staff members to share occupational questions and get to know others walking in the faith. I shared with Pastor Mark this chapter of the book. I can't remember what transpired that brought me to send him this particular chapter, but he wrote back and asked: "Was that the Gonzales church you were writing about?" I told him "Yes, it was." To my surprise, it was another God appointment: Pastor Mark had been the pastor of this church before Pastor Glynn and Connie!

Pastor Mark shared with me how he struggled for fourteen years in this church and felt he couldn't get the breakthrough. He finally moved on to a border town and became the pastor there. What surprises me was his account of a vision he had while pastoring this church in Gonzales. One day he had an open-eyed vision of a column of fire emanating from the sky above and descending right down upon the building. It was a destiny vision! It showed him God's plans and intent for Gonzales, Texas. Destiny visions and dreams may take up to ten and sometimes as long as twenty-five years in the making before they become reality. I was in shock to meet Pastor Mark. He shared with me things God wanted me to know for a purpose I don't understand yet.

The Rest of the Story

I was excited for that night! I arrived at the church right at six o'-clock ready for prayer time. I knew the routine. This church was also a Christian school. The second floor of the building was where the classrooms were. By looking at the small desks and chairs, we had to be in a second- or third-grade classroom. Shuffling a few things around, we made room for fifteen to twenty people. We entered into intercession for that night's meeting. Clearing my mind, I went from an outward reflection of my day into an inner reflection to connect in communion with the Holy Spirit. I so much wanted the Holy Spirit to come and show up like I have seen Him do in numerous dreams. I was pleading with Father God to open the heavens that night and pour out a fresh wave of glory that would change lives forever.

I don't know about you, but for me, being experiential and spiritually sensitive, when I have encounters with the Lord it always takes me upward in the knowledge of God. I don't want any pastor to get nervous here, as we discuss God "out of the box." Our God is a God of order! His ways are not our ways! When He shows up, the enemy rallies his troops and a battle line is drawn. There are times when the manifestations of the Holy Spirit show up. It looks like chaos to us. We must know the Scriptures to hear the Shepherd's voice. We must also know His actions apart from the enemy's distractions that deceive and direct people down the wrong road.

Change of Plans

This night's meeting was different. Pastor Phil stepped out on a limb, and he expected God to show up and touch lives according to His sovereign will. I was hoping the church atmosphere would open and we would all be in the presence of the Lord/Abba Father. I watched as a person-by-person event took place. People were being touched by God and illnesses were being healed. But if it had not been for the testimonies of the healings, you might have missed it. It was as if the Holy Spirit quietly moved about the sanctuary to overshadow this person and that person while the prayers and praise and worship flowed.

Those who received healings were amazed that the God of the universe cared enough for them on such a deeply personal level to heal their bodies. They had wondered if their bodies would ever get back to normal and if they would regain the life they once knew. Several people would be brought to tears in the emotional aftermath, struggling to comprehend what had happened to them. Was this real? "I hoped God would heal me," they would say. "But I didn't think He would do it for me!" Again, I say I love it when God touches a person's life in a tangible way. It confirms that the God of the universe loves them and truly cares for them. This glory experience changes them forever. Their faith and Christian walk takes on new meaning and new direction.

The meeting ended, and many people lingered in the afterglow in this house of God. A flurry of activity was taking place as the hostess prepared the meal for the staff. Tonight, it was Jim and Anita whom I wanted to get to know better. I zeroed in on them for conversation. I then went from wondering if they were the couple God had prepared me to pray with for their spiritual protection to knowing that they were the couple. Now, Lord, please open the door for me to share with them what You had showed me concerning their needs and show me how to begin.

Pastors Phil, Johnny, Glynn, Jim, Shannon, and Lynn were men of God. I admired the work they were doing and their committed desire to see people engulfed in a Holy Spirit revival! These men were impacting my life and challenging me to want more of Jesus and grow in my walk to leadership.

Chapter 18

Day Three of the Conference

I like the morning routine. Up and out for that first cup of coffee and morning briefing with Pastor Phil. On to breakfast and exchanging ministry stories and our encounters with God. We would discuss the details for our targeted prayer for the morning, how to drive there, and the schedule for the speakers. The afternoon of the fourth day was my time spot. I was skipping the group prayer time at the local spot this day to work on my talk. What I like to do is have a printed copy of my message as a handout. Being from the Midwest, I talk very fast. Having a handout allows people to go back and get a second look at an item or point.

Seeing the symbolic messages in the spiritual realm has been an entirely encompassing education. The education continues over the years in order to fully comprehend the details contained in the dreams and visions expressed by God. It is hard work! *The Seer*[1] is another one of my favorite books. I look to Jim Goll as my mentor, by proxy, through his books.

In order to understand this gift from the Lord, I am very well read, but most of my education has come through my relationship with the Holy Spirit. I have always been a self-taught person, always learning new things. What I see in the spirit, I try my best to translate in a way that someone else can grasp. Often the details are hidden in the understanding until the time of release is reached. Many times I will see and learn in hindsight or after the full display unfolds before me. What I see in the spirit I hold on to as being real until it reaches the natural and it is manifested. It is very exciting for me to watch its birth and see it become reality.

Tomorrow, I am going to release my vision of January 20, 2006. I am releasing the "inheritance of the land" shown to me that morning. The time has come, and that will be my message to this region and to the pastors at the conference. I will speak it aloud and decree it into the atmosphere of our world.

Yes, I was nervous. I was not with the group this particular morning so I had some additional free time and planned to go to the Gonzales Museum. Being led by the Holy Spirit often brings adventure and surprises into my life. This city boy from Chicago was standing here in front of the Gonzales Museum because of God and the vision He had shown me years before. This type of adventure is in my DNA. It is exciting following the clues and discovering the things God wants me to know about why He chose this town for me to bring His decree here. Within the doors of the museum is a surprise, to say the least.

People of Faith

Heritage! I didn't see it at first. Walking from showcase to showcase in the museum, I was looking at all the religious material displayed below the glass. There was a printed Bible dating back a couple of centuries. It was a prized family heirloom that had been donated to the museum.

Before the battle for the freedom of Texas, the settlers were very demonstrative in their faith. Beyond a shadow of doubt, the living, breathing spiritual life of God took up residence in the hearts of the early settlers. The town of Gonzales was originally designed to have the main streets laid out in the form of a cross. The core streets are named after saints. Their faith in Jesus Christ rang throughout everything they lived and believed and was the foundation of their lives. By all appearances, in the reflection of their blessing, they lived the first commandment of God. It was truly first in their lives. The realization of the cross being laid out in the town was never to happen, however. One extension of the cross section of the cross was never built. Therefore, looking at a map of Gonzales, you can see a double road area as it looks like a large L.

Let's turn back to historic actions taken by the citizens of Gonzales. Foreigners were encouraged by the nation of Mexico to settle this territory. These were hardy, strong, and determined people. They needed to be hard because of the climate and terrain. These settlers succumbed to rebellion under the tyranny of General Antonio Lopez de Santa Anna. At one time, the Mexican military gave the citizens of Gonzales one small cannon to defend themselves from any invaders.

Now in their rebellion, the Mexican military wanted the cannon back so that in the advent of any conflict between the settlers and the army, the settlers wouldn't have a fighting edge. Thus came the moment of conflict. Battle lines were drawn and the Mexican military were serious about getting their cannon back. From across the field, a high-ranking official shouted, "Return our cannon!" Right there, right then, a battle cry was shouted back with the determination of the people of Gonzales. In one voice they cried in response, "Come and take it!" The battle had begun, and the fight for the freedom of Texas was now underway. The birthplace of freedom for the state of Texas began in Gonzales.

The escalation in the battle encompassed the Alamo. Greatly outnumbered at the Alamo, two hundred settlers went up against four thousand Mexican infantry. The odds were against them. A plea was sent out for reinforcements to all of the surrounding communities. The only help came from Gonzales. Thirty men arrived to engage the Mexican Army in the Battle at the Alamo. In its defeat, only fourteen survivors remained. Women and children were given freedom to relay the tale and the details of the battle in hopes of squelching the drive for freedom. It did not!

General Sam Houston rallied some men and engaged the Mexican Army at its weak point. In the heat of the day, the army was at rest. This battle could have read like the battle Gideon fought with three hundred men, straight out of the Bible. In such total surprise, with confusion and chaos, General Sam Houston defeated this vast army and the freedom of Texas was won. Although this is a very brief synopsis of the full extent of these battles for freedom, I hope you can see that the hand of God was upon the settlers, aiding them in their quest for freedom.

Return Legacy

I'm pulling some points together here. Pastor Phil Corbett, on his grandmother's side, was a "Houston," connecting him directly to Sam Houston. Pastor Phil was engaging in the spiritual battle for Gonzales and the spiritual battle for the state of Texas.

Pastor Glynn was a strong intercessor and was instrumental in setting up the conference and crying out to God for the healing of the land of Gonzales, as in 2 Chronicles 7:14. The Lord had drawn him and his wife, Connie, to return from Alaska to be cutting-edge soldiers in this battle. The Lord used Pastor Glynn's prophetic gifting to affect this region in spiritually plowing the land.

I learned later that Pastor Jim was also on the cutting edge of spiritual change emanating in the region east of Dallas, Texas. Although his church ministered to a small group, Pastor Jim and his wife, Anita, were plowing the land as well for the harvest of the souls of men. I would refer to Pastor Jim as a pastor's pastor. He has longed for a mighty release of living water and grace from Father God above.

Pastor Shannon was a young pastor who sought after his anointing with the Holy Spirit. He saw his desire realized, thrusting him and his family into a new life. He was a new and fresh voice ready to speak the hard words. He doesn't sugarcoat the truth that he shares, but he speaks the truth and worries about the backlash later.

Pastor Johnny, with a pure heart and a desire to please God in his music and songs, reminded me of the priest in the Bible leading the people past the inner courts in the holy of holies. Pastor Johnny was bringing us all beyond the veil into the intimacy of God.

Lastly, Pastor Lynn was the foundation of the conference. Pastor Lynn was the point of spiritual change that he hoped for in hosting this event.

When God shows up, people are healed. Their lives are changed and it becomes the topic of conversation. That was what all the pastors were hoping for. Their hopes were to have the name of Jesus on the tip of every tongue and the center of all the talk in the town.

Is it Because...

There are plenty of places in the Bible where the Lord gives promises to people. He told Abraham his seed would be as the grains of sand on the shoreline. Because of Abraham's faith the Lord blessed his life and legacy. I suspect that because of the love the settlers of Gonzales had for God, He was not done with this town. It had been chosen for the starting point. In my observations, to "inheriting the land," I believe a remnant was saved and others were chosen to usher in what was about to happen in the state of Texas.

Getting back to the day at hand, I was reeling from information overload at the museum. I was taking a moment to allow myself to grasp it all. I needed to return to tonight's focus—Pastor Jim and Anita. The Lord used me at times to remove spiritual hindrances for the purpose of opening up the heavens. It all has to do with who has the spiritual grounds that lay upon the land, or who carries the unrepentant sins and the effects they breed. I have said this before, and I need to attach it to this segment. When the living water dries up, the occult activity comes in its place.

I arrived early at church for the worship service and looked for Pastor Jim and Anita. As they came in the front door, I seized the opportunity to talk with them, asking if they had encountered spiritual warfare in their ministries and lives. Immediately we had a connection. No need to build a bridge for a common starting point! They were praying for God's help and looking for His provision to bring aid to them.

It is generally known that people are dabbling in the occult at an alarming rate. It is like a pyramid scheme. Many are dabblers, just a few tapping in to dangerous power with evil and wielding their skills for the ill of mankind. Pastor Jim found an occult spell attached to the gate out in front of his church. Thinking nothing about it, he removed it from the fence gate and they went on with their lives. But things were not the same. Why? I don't know exactly, but when it was brought out and revealed to me what was happening in their lives, I knew God had a plan.

I asked Pastor Lynn if there was a place where Jim, Anita, and I could go to have quiet prayer. We were directed to the copy room on the second floor. There we prayed for the forgiveness of sin that had allowed an open door for attack. We prayed for the home they lived in, the property it sat on, and we rebuked the spell Jim had found. When we were done, their lives were restored to a safe spiritual environment. The victory was all God's. He brought all of these components together. He alone gets the praise.

I had missed part of the prayer meeting before the service, and I slipped into the room as invisibly as I could. Again we entered into inner reflection to connect with the Holy Spirit, petitioning for an outpouring in tonight's service. We had a good time of prayer. In tonight's service, you could see a relaxed state, a visible display of freedom in the spirit.

The battles for the people of Gonzales had already begun. This time, it was without guns and cannons, for it was not against flesh and blood but against principalities and rulers in high places. An exchange of ownership for the land in the spiritual realm had begun, and where there had been gloom and darkness (see Isaiah 29:18), there is seen liberty and freedom in the hearts and lives of the people. That night more people came forward for prayer, and more people gave their testimony as to what the Lord had done for them. The momentum was building and the excitement was displayed in what was often a dry area. Jesus was again on the tongues of the people's conversations.

During the staff meal, now a familiar gathering, the voices were louder to talk over the crowd and be heard. Laughter was filling the air. The joy of the Lord was being revealed. The peak of the event for me surfaced. I had a full understanding of the message that I would be presenting tomorrow afternoon in the state of Texas. Praise the Lord!

Chapter 19

Fourth Day of the Conference

I felt the weight of responsibility. Most likely it was self-imposed. I wanted to give my best presentation and accurately convey the message the Lord showed me to the best of my ability. I was learning about speaking in churches and being up in front. It is a praise story for God. The evolution of my progress was unbelievable. My life developed from being a person one step from the door whenever I was in church to gaining enough strength from the Lord to be able to share my deep relationship with Jesus in front of a crowd. It burns within me to share the Gospel of Jesus Christ with others. I long to help Christians climb higher in their walk with the Lord. Twenty-nine years of preparation and education by the Holy Spirit have developed my testimony. The time has come to step out and trust God.

In preparation, I ran through all the details of my vision and how I would present my message. I have much appreciation for pastors and their sermon preparation for Sunday mornings. I have learned through experience that it takes me about ten hours to prepare sixty minutes of speaking material, and pastors do this every week.

I invited my brother-in-law, Ed, to be in the group for some additional support. Ed was leaving for home right after I spoke. He would have his camper and pickup out front on the street. I was glad he placed my message high on his priority list. To my surprise, having family with me was taking on a new perspective. My bond with Ed built up my strength and confidence.

There was a flurry of activity in the church that morning. Pastor Phil asked me if I would mind speaking in the morning session as Pastor Shannon needed additional time to prepare. "I'm ready to go," I told him. He waved over Pastor Lynn and he asked me a few questions on where I would like to stand. "On the platform, behind the podium, or would you like a music stand on the floor just in front of the seat?" he asked me. A heartfelt feeling arose that I would rather be on the floor closer to those I would be speaking to. I didn't feel comfortable with the thought of being on the platform. Maybe when I got better at this, I would use the podium, but for now being on the floor suited me just fine.

Stepping into a New Role

My notes and Bible were on the seat next to me. The worship team began to play and my phobia was overcome. During the second song I noticed the surge of the Holy Spirit's power wrapped around my legs. It was comforting and confirming I knew then we would be facing the pastors and guests together. It was time! Pastor Lynn introduced me and I took my place. My first action was to ask Pastor Phil if he would pass out the copies of notes I had prepared.

I had it all laid out, beginning with my experiential life in Christ, leading into the main point: "the vision." My thoughts were, *Will I make it through this time without crying?* So far, when I get to the point of explaining the supernatural reunion with my precious daughters, I get all choked up in the emotion. It was exactly how Jesus feels about His Bride, the Church—how each church, or daughter, is a part of the Bride of Christ. This is the most important point in the drawing out of the message to the "inheritance of the land."

Because this chapter is the pivotal point in this book, I have taken several days to prepare. I have been seeking the Lord, spending time in prayer and asking my wife to pray with me. I want the Lord to bless me with talent and craftsmanship like He did so many times in the Bible stories. In this environment, the thought entered my mind that I have the opportunity to give a new and updated message. It has been nearly two years since the release of the vision. I have grown and come into new understandings about it. It only seems appropriate to start new with you.

Faith

Faith is a "trusting commitment of one person in another, particularly of a person in God. Faith is the central concept of Christianity. One may be called a Christian only if one has faith" (*Holman Bible Dictionary*).

According to the *World English Dictionary*, faith is a

1. strong or unshakeable belief in something, esp. without proof or evidence

2. a specific system of religious beliefs: the Jewish faith

3. Christianity: trust in God and in His actions and promises

4. a conviction of the truth of certain doctrines of religion, esp. when this is not based on reason

5. complete confidence or trust in a person, remedy, etc.

6. any set of firmly held principles or beliefs

In my own words, faith is an understanding in our minds; a position in our hearts that we decide to take. It will play a pivotal role in the realization of the vision of inheriting the land. To read it alone is to appreciate a good story. To believe that God sent it for you to read and have faith in, is to receive it and all God intends for you to have through its realization.

Little Children—Greatest in the Kingdom

At that time the disciples came to Jesus and asked, "Who, then, is the greatest in the kingdom of heaven?" (Matthew 18:1–5)

He called a little child to him and placed the child among them. And he said: "Truly I tell you, unless you change and become like little children, you will never enter the kingdom of heaven. Therefore, whoever takes the lowly position of this child is the greatest in the kingdom of heaven. And whoever welcomes one such child in my name welcomes me."

A critical issue in the vision that I am about to share with you is, "Will you be able to receive it as a child would?" I like what *Matthew Henry's Commentary*[1] has to say about this verse, and I have decided to include it. It says:

> The necessity of humility, His preface is solemn, and commands both attention and assent; Verily I say unto you, I, the Amen, the faithful Witness, say it, Except ye be converted, and become as little children, ye shall not enter into the kingdom of heaven.
>
> What it is that he requires and insists upon? First, "You must be converted, you must be of another mind, and in another frame and temper, must have other thoughts, both of yourselves and of the kingdom of heaven, before you be fit for a place in it. The pride, ambition, and affectation of honor and dominion, which appear in you, must be repented of, mortified, and reformed, and you must come to yourselves."

As I read this, it occurred to me in a roundabout way, we need the simplicity of a child's heart where faith is at its peak.

Our arena in the United States, with all of our technology and cultural prowess, diminishes the acceptability of the true reality of a vision in our everyday life. I do not think anyone would dispute the spiritual decline we are experiencing. However, as in the illustration of a teeter-totter, whenever one side goes down, the other side goes up. With the spiritual decline and lack of morals, ethics, and godly standards, comes the advent of a new move of God. Through a spiritual increase in a new and unexpected way, we see a tsunami wave of the Holy Spirit arriving in places that were previously devoid of spiritual life.

Now it is time to share with you my vision that I shared at the conference. The stage is set with my prepared thoughts to hold in mind as you read its accounts and my discoveries afterward. Here we go:

A Vision of Inheriting the Land
in the Southern United States

Early in the morning on January 20, 2006, I had a vision. It was one of the most powerful experiences I have ever had in the Lord. I often quote the apostle Paul when he said, "I know a man, whether he was in the body or out of the body I don't know." Paul was talking about himself in the third-person reference. He was trying to explain a spiritual visitation he had had. That was how I felt about this vision, except I know I wasn't in the body. The Lord had taken me somewhere else.

One moment I was asleep in my room, and the next I was in an office. In this office I could only see one wall. I have come to discover, years later, that the building material I had seen making up the back wall was hewn stone. There are several types and finishes of hewn stone, and this was very finely textured with a light gray color. The stones were cut in squares two feet by two feet. The lay lines were so tight between the stones that no gaps could be seen. About six feet up the wall were fluorescent light fixtures. Their horizontal position was illuminating the wall and reflecting off the ceiling. I noticed that the room was well lit.

Standing directly in front of the wall at a distance of maybe seven or eight feet, by and large the room was empty except for a desk off to my left. It was a wooden desk of dark mahogany and looked very expensive. Immediately I noticed that I was not alone. I was with my two daughters. The oldest was age five and my youngest was age three. (At the time of the vision their ages were actually twenty-six and twenty-four.) Please bear with me here. I am trying to describe a spiritual event that was truly real. It was really my daughters, the way they were just at those ages. I was thirty-one when they were five and three.

I had this same experience years ago, being in the presence of my younger daughter, so when I stepped into this vision I understood what was happening. I lost no time knowing I had just minutes to be with them. I quickly started to play with them, rough-housing like we loved to do. Then a man entered the scene from my left and introduced himself. I was borderline rude to him; my total focus was on my daughters. My first thought was, *Leave me alone, pal, so I can be with my girls!* He started talking and conveyed to me that it was for them that this meeting was taking place. That was why we are all there together.

My emotions and spirit had just gone into overload. I have loved being their father. It was the best times of my life. I was overwhelmed to be in their presence; my love for them spilled over to controlled sobs caught in my throat. Tears filled my eyes with the joy of it all. Really, I wanted to scoop them both up into my arms and smother them with kisses. However, there was a reason for this to be happening. The girls' advocate was going to give us a message.

He began to explain to me that he was an advocate on behalf of the girls, and we needed to talk about some very serious legal matters. *Okay,* I thought, *you have my attention.* I was switching into the father mode. The girls' advocate was an elderly man, probably in his early seventies. He was strong in character and walked with social affluence. I could see that he was an educated man. His mannerisms were very polished, and his speech was articulate but not lofty. He stepped over to his desk and reached for a cardboard tube that held a rolled-up picture. Popping the end open, he guided out a paper roll and then set the tube back on the desktop. He began to talk to me. He said, "Your daughters are going to have an inheritance!" I immediately had a flashback to my teenage years when I had inherited money from my grandfather. My sisters and I each inherited two hundred dollars. A first impression came out of the reflection in my own life. *So,* I thought, *what's all this big deal?* I placed the level of the importance of the meeting on a very low scale.

I was now clearly in the role of their legal guardian. He was leading me to comprehend all the details important to their inheritance. Although my daughters were very young, he was giving them respect as if they were royalty. In one fluid motion he moved from standing and went to a kneeling position. He now had one hand on the floor holding the edge of the paper while with the other hand he unraveled it. We were going to conduct business on the floor so the girls could see all that was going on. Simultaneously, I lay down on my stomach. Then my younger daughter quickly lay down on my back as little children will do with their dads (that sweet, connected love, no barriers between father and child). My older daughter seemed to be a bit standoffish and lay down about an arm's reach away. As she lay down on her back, I wanted her to be part of the activities so I reached over, grabbing her left forearm, and gently pulled her nearer to us. It was all about them, and she needed to be involved even if she didn't understand.

I was stunned to see the image of a map as the paper was rolling open. It was one of those topographical maps with the boundaries of the states clearly defined. Uh-oh! I was not in the mental position I need to be for the sake of the girls! *This was no small inheritance, but how could this be?* In a snap I was on high alert to comprehend what was happening. The girls and I were lying with the view of the bottom of the map, the southern states. The lawyer, still on his knees, had his weight resting on his right hand. Once the map was completely open, there was no doubt, it was a full map of the United States of America.

With a sweeping motion of his left hand and his fingertips upon the map, he began to verbally communicate the territory that the girls would inherit. Stressing the enormity of the land mass, he used three repetitious strokes across the map. His fingertips began by touching central eastern Texas and from there his hand swept into Louisiana, and continued upward into Tennessee and Kentucky and on into the Ohio Valley. Shocked and dismayed, I thought, *How can this be?* Then he shifted his weight onto his left hand and began a sweeping motion now with his right hand. Starting in Central Texas he swept upward and into Oklahoma and beyond into Nebraska and finished in the state of Colorado. What can I say, I was at a loss for words.

Reaching up to the top of his desk, he grabbed a group of papers and set them down on the map before me. They were legal documents that needed to be signed. He handed me a pen, and it was as if I were watching in the third-person view. I saw myself signing my full legal name on the line he had indicated. I was signing these documents as the girls' legal guardian. The mission was now complete! It was ending; the vision was coming to a close and I could feel it. I felt myself begin to panic! Wait, I didn't want to leave the girls yet. Did I fully understand how I was going to be their guardian in this inheritance? My eyes quickly searched the map for anything of importance and there it was. Printed upon the right-hand corner of the map was a large block set of numbers: 376.

As quickly as the vision began, it was over. I was lying in my bed, half-asleep, but awake enough to still feel my experience. My heart was aching, full of joy one moment and then sorrow the next. A steady stream of tears flowed from my eyes and down my cheeks. I was so moved by this experience that hours passed as I tried to remember every detail and commit it all to memory. I truly would like to put into words how wonderful it was to be in that room with my girls and be their father again, even if it was only for a few precious minutes. I loved every second we were together.

376

One of the first things I wanted to know was what the number 376 stood for and why it was important. When I had a chance, I sat down in front of the computer and brought up the Google search engine. I put in the search window the number 376 and looked to see what came up. I explored page after page of references connected with that number. Nothing seemed to make sense. Often what will happen during this kind of search is that a link will lead you to a new branch that leads you to another link, and somehow, you guessed it, I was lost and didn't know how I had arrived at the website I was currently on. My head hurt!

What happens with me during a search like this kind on the web is that my thoughts are expanded, and I enter a new search with new information I have learned. It is all about how to ask the question in a search engine. It eventually brought me to *Strong's Hebrew Lexicon*! Until this time I had never heard of a Hebrew or Greek lexicon. The *Strong's Concordance* uses numbers for word locations in the Bible, making it easier to find that reference. "Aha!" Finally I had my answer. I brought up a website for the Hebrew lexicon and entered the number 376 to see what the concordance would say about it. A plethora of material came up. Reading each definition, the letter E grabbed my attention. It simply meant: "mankind"! Now I had it, the inheritance was about people.

My next challenge was to understand what the symbolism of my daughters represented. I found it in Psalm 48:11: "Let Mount Zion be glad! Let the daughters of Judah rejoice because of Your [righteous] judgments." *Matthew Henry's Commentary* on Psalm 48 connects the daughters of Judah with the Church. So there I had another piece of the puzzle. My daughters symbolized individual churches across the southern states of America. In the natural flow of questioning, I asked, "Why were my daughters at the ages three and five?"

I also like *Matthew Henry's Concise Commentary* on Matthew 18:3:

Our Lord set a little child before them, solemnly assuring them, that unless they were converted and made like little children, they could not enter his kingdom. Children, when very young, do not desire authority, do not regard outward distinctions, are free from malice, are teachable, and willingly dependent on their parents. It is true that they soon begin to show other dispositions, and other ideas are taught them at an early age; but these are marks of childhood, and render them proper emblems of the lowly minds of true Christians.

I posed a question to the Lord: *Are the churches to believe Your message in the vision like a little child?* Again I thought to ask another question: *Lord, what will they inherit?* Those answers would come later.

Fellow Christians

The main reason I have written this book was to connect with my brothers and sisters in Christ in a personal way. I want to be transparent in my walk with Jesus and show a path of development leading me to hopefully being credible. Without that credibility and seeing God behind the man, it will be just a good story. I am hoping the Holy Spirit within you gives witness to God moving in me. We need revival in America (a new move of God). Is this vision our God's way of showing us that He has a plan? I have committed my life to work for the Lord and respond to His lead. This is concerning the actual manifestation of the message held in the vision. It is only as real as the faith within each heart.

Seeing a church symbolically represented as a daughter of the Lord may be hard for a people to understand. I struggled with the meaning of why the Lord would use my little girls to be the stand-in for the churches spread across Texas and the southern United States. The pastor is the figurehead of the Lord Jesus Christ to the members, and the total sum of the ministry was seen as a daughter in the vision? Why else would the Lord use my two girls?

I have wondered about the inheritance aspect of the vision, as well, and how it will come to be in the natural. Sometimes, even after I have sought the Lord endlessly, the fullness of understanding only comes in the hour of His completion, and I see it! At this point in time can I share the details of the inheritance and what it will mean for us? No! It is yet to come. Now it is time to release it.

To all of you who are reading this book, this inheritance is for an individual, as well. In a chapter yet to come, I have prayers to help you enter into this inheritance. For years, I have been praying with people on a one-on-one basis. It is the position of our hearts that is ultimately important. I have encountered many people who are hurting and in need of God's help. Those who have lost jobs and homes have contacted the ministry (NeedHimMinistries.org) to have someone pray with them. I led them to rededicate their lives to Jesus. They had left their first love in Jesus and drifted away and into ruin. I share with them Psalm 107 and tell them that their repentant heart is one motion away to being united with the Father again. Take heart, the Lord is very near!

As quickly as it had begun, my time of speaking came to a close. It is one of those times when you know you had invisible help guiding you through to the end. As I left the front of the church, a new set of questions began. How did people receive the message I had released? It was now time for our lunch break, and I knew Ed would be leaving so I sought him out immediately. Together we walked out to his truck and trailer, and I asked him how he thought it went. To my surprise, he told me he could have listed to me a lot longer. He enjoyed the message and was interested in the spiritual life he felt flowing in it. He longed to know more. I was sad to see Ed go.

During the lunch break I felt relief knowing my portion was now complete, and I could relax and enjoy the remainder of the conference. I was grateful to Pastor Phil for making this day possible. I was grateful to all the pastors who invested in my time in Gonzales, Texas. I love the pure adventure through God's guiding hands and looked forward to the healing service tonight to see what God would do. The road to Gonzales was now over and the road to understanding God's releasing His new move was just beginning.

A new phase begins at this point. The mechanics of this inheritance will unfold. In the following chapters are things you will want to know. This new move of God will be affecting many people. Will it be enough to stay the hand of God in what lies ahead?

Chapter 20

2 Chronicles 7:14

If my people, who are called by my name, will humble themselves and pray and seek my face and turn from their wicked ways, then I will hear from heaven, and I will forgive their sin and will heal their land (2 Chronicles 7:14).

There is a growing interest in this verse in our day. It is not hard to see that America is on a downward spiral in its spiritual life. Ethics and moral standards based on Christian principles are dropping. We are seeing a dramatic rise in serious violence and crime. For Christians, it brings a cry within our hearts for our Father God to help us in our need. Mentally and intellectually, we comprehend the seriousness in our cultural decline. It is not until we reach the heartfelt expression that it reaches the ear of Father God.

What are the mechanics of 2 Chronicles 7:14? You've read this far into the book, so you see that I am an experiential Christian and I look at things from a mechanical point of view. That is why I always ask God to help me understand things in a way I can grasp it.

Heart expressions are not everyday occurrences. We live life in our day-to-day routine. We enjoy those moments of heart expression like taking pride in our children's accomplishments or receiving unconditional love from our spouses just when we need it. Expressions of the heart are terms of endearment for those we love.

When our lives are out of control, God intervenes. His perfect timing and perfect solution or provision comes to our rescue. Our hearts will then take over and respond with feelings of gratitude and love toward our God. A special gift was sent from Father God. The mutual love makes another connection. There you go—the mechanics of the heart! We are so thankful.

For days we might be experiencing difficulties. Some of us can take a lot of pain and frustration, and we pull up our boot straps and keep on going. We might even be stubborn and stiff-necked toward God. But the moment we turn our hearts to Him and cry out, He rushes in to meet our needs and cover us in His love.

Humbling ourselves before God is an entirely different issue. As Americans, we are used to being independent, especially in the area of finances. Our jobs and income are so regular that we often take them for granted. We have increased knowledge from the abundance of higher education available to us. Our knowledge sometimes has separated us from God through reasoning and rationalization. We have conquered illness and diseases. We have split the atom and can see into the depths of our universe.

Our higher levels of thinking can now become a hindrance to needing a higher power, God. In our ability to think we have lost our way to seeing spiritual truths and how our world works on spiritual applications and not worldly wisdom. For example, you may have fallen through the cracks of the declining workforce and lost your job. Because of the economic downturn, a turbulent atmosphere between 2009 and 2011 has resulted. You may have come to realize that your worldly wisdom and knowledge has not kept you out of the downward spiral. Your degrees (BS, MBA, or even a doctorate) may not be as satisfying as you had thought it would be. Your happiness and satisfaction with life is really low on the scale right now.

Then there comes a turning point when we see our need for God. This is the threshold of expressing a humbled heart toward Him. You come to a point of being willing to turn from being proud, independent, and possibly callous-hearted to switching to a new position. This will allow your heart to be submissive to the Lord.

Due to the economy, many businesses have had to adapt new policies and procedures. This brought many changes. I haven't welcomed many of these changes in my own job. We are experiencing increased workloads. I am spoiled. I have had some of the best customers and buildings to work in my entire career. With the new changes, I have to go into buildings that I wouldn't send my worst enemy into. Two weeks ago, I made my first visit to a Chicago hotel. I was brought to a door that would lead me to the elevator machine room. I needed to have access to maintain the elevator according to the contract. I cracked the door open only about two inches, which was just enough to turn on the lights and peek in. I wanted to see if anything moved inside. (You know—like a critter.) I stepped in and immediately I felt sick. I wanted to say, "The heck with this!" and walk out. But I need this job. I felt, in my heart, a humbling as I went inside! I submitted to this, just as Jesus submitted Himself to the Father. God knows what is happening here and it is no surprise to Him. I walked out of that hotel being very grateful and feeling humble in many ways.

America is in a downward spiral. We are going to be humbled in a multiple of ways. As individuals, in our churches, our factories, our jobs, in finances, and in our government, we will be humbled.

Psalm 107

Give thanks to the Lord, for he is good; his love endures forever. Let the redeemed of the Lord tell their story—those he redeemed from the hand of the foe, those he gathered from the lands, from east and west, from north and south. Some wandered in desert wastelands, finding no way to a city where they could settle. They were hungry and thirsty, and their lives ebbed away. Then they cried out to the Lord in their trouble, and he delivered them from their distress. He led them by a straight way to a city where they could settle. Let them give thanks to the Lord for his unfailing love and his wonderful deeds for mankind, for he satisfies the thirsty and fills the hungry with good things.

Some sat in darkness, in utter darkness, prisoners suffering in iron chains, because they rebelled against God's commands and despised the plans of the Most High. So he subjected them to bitter labor; they stum-

bled, and there was no one to help. Then they cried to the Lord in their trouble, and he saved them from their distress. He brought them out of darkness, the utter darkness, and broke away their chains. Let them give thanks to the Lord for his unfailing love and his wonderful deeds for mankind, for he breaks down gates of bronze and cuts through bars of iron.

Some became fools through their rebellious ways and suffered affliction because of their iniquities. They loathed all food and drew near the gates of death. Then they cried to the Lord in their trouble, and he saved them from their distress. He sent out his word and healed them; he rescued them from the grave. Let them give thanks to the Lord for his unfailing love and his wonderful deeds for mankind. Let them sacrifice thank offerings and tell of his works with songs of joy.

Some went out on the sea in ships; they were merchants on the mighty waters. They saw the works of the Lord, his wonderful deeds in the deep. For he spoke and stirred up a tempest that lifted high the waves. They mounted up to the heavens and went down to the depths; in their peril their courage melted away. They reeled and staggered like drunkards; they were at their wits' end. Then they cried out to the Lord in their trouble, and he brought them out of their distress. He stilled the storm to a whisper; the waves of the sea were hushed. They were glad when it grew calm, and he guided them to their desired haven. Let them give thanks to the Lord for his unfailing love and his wonderful deeds for mankind. Let them exalt him in the assembly of the people and praise him in the council of the elders.

He turned rivers into a desert, flowing springs into thirsty ground, and fruitful land into a salt waste, because of the wickedness of those who lived there. He turned the desert into pools of water and the parched ground into flowing springs; there he brought the hungry to live, and they founded a city where they could settle. They sowed fields and planted vineyards that yielded a fruitful harvest; he blessed them, and their numbers greatly increased, and he did not let their herds diminish.

Then their numbers decreased, and they were humbled by oppression, calamity and sorrow; he who pours contempt on nobles made them wander in a trackless waste. But he lifted the needy out of their affliction and increased their families like flocks. The upright see and rejoice, but all the wicked shut their mouths.

Let the one who is wise heed these things and ponder the loving deeds of the Lord.

I love this psalm! Within this psalm, there is the hidden cycle of human behavior. To live by God's commands it takes commitment and dedication. Living our lives in this manner brings many blessings from God. He leads us to prosperity and comfort. By the second, third, and fourth generation we lose why we walk in the ways of God. We start to become independent in our hearts and thinking. We begin to go our own way, and ultimately it leads to doing anything that is right in our own eyes. (see Judges 21:25). When this happens, our relationship with God, Jesus, and the Holy Spirit is no longer in the top spot of our hearts and lives. The pinnacle has been reached. It might only be one thing that starts us downward in the spiritual blessing of God.

The Lord will send on you curses, confusion and rebuke in everything you put your hand to, until you are destroyed and come to sudden ruin because of the evil you have done in forsaking him (Deuteronomy 28:20).

Is America now feeling the judgment from God? I believe that when we move away from Him, He moves away from us. I make the point here that the word *forsake* is so important because it starts everything moving downhill. It is the beginning of lesser times. Psalm 107 shows that they came to a place of humbling themselves, and Father God was immediately there to start a change in an upward move again.

Repentance

We need to understand what sin does to our lives and what corporate sin does to our land. The effects of sin upon the land bring open doors to the demonic and legal rights we call "grounds." Until those grounds are forgiven, there can be no transfer of ownership in the spiritual realm. It takes many human attempts to resolve the problems. People will finally arrive at the heartfelt expression of understanding that there is no humanly way out of their troubles. At what point will we be willing to admit our need for God?

Repentance, a spiritual event within our hearts, only comes from a release of grace given to those who seek after His face. A key point is the acknowledgment that we are sinners. We are not to be prideful children, stiff-necked and rebellious. We are converted to seeing our need of a Father and Savior, our God who changes all things with a spoken word. We need to seek Him with our entire heart, mind, and soul. We need to humble ourselves before Him. Then He will release that grace to us in our act of repentance. Then we can see!

I received a call from a young woman just three weeks ago. In a revival meeting in Alaska, she opened her heart to the Holy Spirit. That night, in her home, she had a vision. The Lord revealed her own sins in the light of a holy God. It is a spiritual event only God can give when we see with our spiritual eyes and feel it in the innermost parts of our hearts. Then we grasp the difference. Once the apostle Paul saw his sins in the light of God's holiness, he referred to his life as "filthy rags." Jesus paid a price for our salvation and the forgiveness of our sins. Being exposed to the holiness of God puts an enormous price tag on Jesus' sacrifice. We can't understand this unless the Lord reveals it to us. And this is something all Christians need to see and experience.

Groundwork Laid—Pastor Becky's Story

What is the new work God has planned for us to receive? I shared with you the vision of January 20, 2006. The main tenet is the daughters of the Church are inheriting the land! What does that look like in reality? The illustration comes in an example of what God did in the life of Pastor Becky. Pastor Becky lives in Louisiana and co-pastors with her brother. When I spoke and released the vision at the pastor's conference in Gonzales, Texas, Pastor Becky caught it. In a conversation by e-mail, Pastor Becky shared with me her feelings in response to being at the conference. She wrote, "I feel in awe of the godly men and women here. They inspired me to desire more of Jesus and His glory!" Pastor Becky's heart was in a place that was ready to receive from the Lord.

Two weeks after the conference, I called all the pastors I had made contact with. I was anxious to see how they were doing and if any changes had come to their ministry. When I talked with Pastor Becky, I discovered that the presence of God had erupted in her church. Caught by surprise with the advent of the presence of God, within weeks she and her brother invited a host of pastors to come and help evaluate the change. They wanted to validate this new move they were experiencing. In their Sunday service, the presence of God was so strong that at times visitors would come forward asking, "What must I do to become a child of God?" The pastors shared God's plan for salvation through Jesus' death on the cross.

I would like you to understand what the Lord was doing on behalf of Pastor Becky. Behind the scenes, in the spiritual realm, He was showing me in dreams what He was doing on her behalf. That first night, after speaking with Pastor Becky on the phone, I had this dream. I began to see myself on a vast, open plain covered with wild grass no more than a foot tall. It is odd in retrospect—there were no weeds anywhere. As far as the eye could see, the grass was dancing in the breeze. To my right appeared an Indian warrior in full battle dress. A spear was in his left hand with the end of the spear resting on the ground. He was atop an Appaloosa pony that had brown and white patches of color upon its hide. He was about two hundred feet away from me. Clearly we were looking at each other, and I wondered what was going to happen next. In an instant, the Indian warrior dug his heels into the belly of the pony, spurring him forward in my direction. At a full gallop he closed the gap in seconds. I immediately lay down in the grass trying to make it harder for him to see me. It all took place so fast; I lay parallel to his approach with my head to the right. He came at me from the right. When he was within a few feet of me, he thrust his spear in my direction! It landed between my left arm and ribs, just nicking my side.

I suffered a slight wound as the spearhead grazed me. I woke up from this dream that was bigger than life itself. My heart was racing fast. I have survived two heart attacks. And I tell you that I definitely was in a panic. I had no trouble remembering the details of the dream. I lay in bed praying and interceding for Pastor Becky's region.

Within days I called her again to ask about the history of her town. I asked her about the chance of knowing the historical background on the Indian occupation. She quickly answered me by saying yes. Knowing the spiritual practices of the Native American Indians, I began to pray for the removal of the sins upon the land associated with their beliefs. However, I think the Lord had already stepped in and removed the principalities to bring healing to the land.

I had a second dream in connection with Pastor Becky. This was directed more to what God was now going to do in her personal life and family. As the dream unfolded, I saw myself in the backyard of her house. I was there looking about the grounds and stayed mainly in an open-sided toolshed that was positioned on the right end of the house. It was just off the side of the sliding-glass doors. The door was open and a slight breeze was gently moving the drapes. My attention was changed as I saw some movement in the distance. Two mature tigers were approaching the rear of the house. Coming near with the demeanor of not having a care in the world, they reached about ten feet directly behind the sliding-glass door. The tigers glanced at me and then started toward the door. Their intention was to enter the house.

I watched as a man stepped up to the door with Pastor Becky next to him. From within the house, together they slid the glass door closed and locked it. Undeterred, the tigers were still approaching the door with the intent on entering, just like they had done so many times before, but not this time. I picked up a long-handled shovel. Swinging it swiftly and with precision, I hit the leading tiger on the side of the nose closest to the door and away from the building. Stunned, the tiger shot me a glance and began toward the door again. Without a thought, I took a second swing with the shovel as I hit the tiger right in the same spot. Now I had the tiger's full attention. He looked at me as if to say, *Who the heck are you? No one has ever interfered with my coming and going before!* I was standing a mere six feet away from the tigers with only a long-handled shovel in my hand. I woke up. My heart was going to explode, it was beating so hard.

What was happening in the life of Pastor Becky? Two principalities had total access to her home and family. Now with inheriting the land, Jesus took ownership of the land, restricting all demonic hindrances. Jesus was now the protector and owner. He was now actively healing the land of any and all spiritual predators. One of the first things Pastor Becky began to experience was the salvation of two of her children and one grandchild. One of the invited, visiting pastors was staying at Pastor Becky's home for two nights. He was there to try and help them understand what was happening in the church. Pastor Phil and his wife stayed at Pastor Becky's home for two nights, as well. He told me, "Tom, it was like sleeping under an open heaven. I never experienced anything like it! There was a wonderful peace there."

I had thought long and hard about the symbolism of the long-handled shovel. It is the shovel of choice for the gardeners. It is easier on the back when working the ground in the garden, moving dirt, any type of dirt. Then came the message: Jesus was working the spiritual soil of Pastor Becky's life and family. The Lord was bringing healing to the land! Now I can see the applications to the Scripture above. But wait, there's more.

In yet another dream, the Lord showed me, He went to Pastor Becky's day job, as well. There too He began to work in the spiritual arena of her job, taking control of that environment. Within days of coming home from Gonzales, Pastor Becky received for herself the promise in this new move of God. It was in all areas of her life. Jesus was now taking possession from the enemy.

The region of Louisiana where Pastor Becky lives not only has the spiritual heritage of the Native Americans, it also has that of the French settlers. The French in her area were heavily into occult activity, and for several centuries evil reigned throughout the area. It was no small feat to the transfer of ownership of the land. Jesus was turning the region upside down.

Two years later, the revival presence of the Lord they had in the beginning had now diminished, but the ripples of the transferred ownership had continued to expand in increasing ways. There have been changed lives as a result of the revival presence of God. Pastor Becky's church, family, and workplace are impacting the community, and it is spreading into the region. Lives continue to be impacted for Jesus, and the demographics are changing. It is the battleground for the Kingdom of God, and His army is advancing one step at a time. This is only the beginning of the realization of my vision. I now asked the Lord to help me comprehend how this would grow into the huge inheritance that He had shown me in the vision.

In yet another dream, from a position of high above the earth at night, I looked down upon the southern region of the United States. The glow from the city lights was breathtaking and beautiful. In an instant, out of the center of one of those cities, it looked like a kernel of popcorn that popped, shooting high into the atmosphere. The arc was falling back to earth and multiplying. It went into an additional five cities. From the same location, the center of the city, another kernel exploded and shot upward. This time the trajectory took on a new direction and landed in a neighboring city. I watched as five kernels popped again from that city. Each time they were expanding the amount of cities they were hitting. This continued, just like popping corn in the microwave. From my vantage point I now saw arcing popcorn kernels jumping all over the state of Texas and then into Louisiana. I could understand now just how God intended to carry out His plan. This would bring about the new move of His daughters of the Church into inheriting the land.

There will be many struggles ahead, adding to the numbers of already hurting people in our land. The deeper we go into struggles and pain, the more willing we are to let go of the life we live. Are we ready for the journey that Jesus will set us on for our own restoration? Will we be willing to turn from our sinful ways and embrace the holiness of God?

Yesterday I had a call from a woman in her mid-forties. She was in so much pain; her life had fallen apart and she had nowhere to turn. Sobbing with choked-up words that sounded more like slurs, she called for help. Spiritually, only Jesus Christ can bring the kind of help she needed. I long to see hundreds and thousands of churches, daughters of the Bride of Christ, embrace this vision so that they too can inherit the land. I call all my brothers and sisters in the Lord. Together we can be blessed as citizens and as an entire nation. I believe we will see a restoration of ethics and morals based on the life of Jesus Christ, not secular wisdom and empty, false religions. We can walk in the security it brings. We can continue to enjoy the freedom and liberty flowing out of God's applications. We can see a major reduction of crime and violence that comes from being "One Nation under God."

Chapter 21

Sowing Seeds

Recently I had an "aha" moment. I have been sowing seeds for decades, and they have been lying in the soil. In the Body of Christ there are many members. There are different gifts and talents used in the Kingdom of God. Some sow, others water, and then there are those who cultivate. Finally we have the reapers. These are the steps of development of the seed from beginning to end. All of these expressions are word pictures for the beginning, seeing the realization of people being birthed into the Kingdom of God and becoming born again. The Word of God, the Bible, is where the seed comes from and springs to life when mixed with the human heart and faith.

I have spent years trying to understand how this whole thing works, the "second birth," or what some say, "born again," as it is mentioned below in John 3:3–8.

> *Jesus replied, "Very truly I tell you, no one can see the kingdom of God unless they are born again."*
>
> *"How can someone be born when they are old?" Nicodemus asked. "Surely they cannot enter a second time into their mother's womb to be born!"*
>
> *Jesus answered, "Very truly I tell you, no one can enter the kingdom of God unless they are born of water and the Spirit. Flesh gives birth to flesh, but the Spirit gives birth to spirit. You should not be surprised at my saying, 'You must be born again.' The wind blows wherever it*

pleases. You hear its sound, but you cannot tell where it comes from or where it is going. So it is with everyone born of the Spirit."

In verse 6 it says, "flesh gives birth to flesh." The coming together of a man and woman, two elements together, the sperm from the man and the egg within the woman cause a new life to begin. I would say we can all grasp this illustration! But the second part of verse 6 is the difficult portion: "But the Spirit gives birth to spirit," and this all lies within the invisible spiritual realm where our human eyes cannot see.

Doorway

Sometimes I see myself as a slow learner. It took me a long time to see that the functions of our human heart, our emotions, are spiritual acts. Our feelings lie within the spiritual side of our lives connected with our souls that are everlasting. The human heart is the doorway to the spiritual realm. This is where the seed of God is placed. It is within our emotional hearts. The first part of the process to becoming born again emanates from our emotional hearts. The next important ingredient is the Holy Spirit. No one can be born again aside from the presence of the Holy Spirit. This is a key component. The Holy Spirit represents the spiritual life that will be placed within us at the point of conversion. The next vital piece is God's plan for salvation for the human race, told within the books of the Bible.

The spiritual realm is not like our world. God is in the spiritual realm along with Jesus, the Holy Spirit, and the angels. The other side is evil, including all of the fallen angels that fell with Satan. All beings in the spiritual realm are not human, nor do they think or act like humans. This understanding came to me while I was seeking a deeper understanding of evil. Evil just didn't make sense to me. People hurting people and wanting to control and do harm to others never clicked in to my "knowing." Oh, I have been hurt and abused. Why does such pain exist? It just didn't make sense to me. So, I sought God to help me understand.

I like parameters and boundaries in my life and in the world. It brings me safety and stability in my spirit and mind. The spiritual realm is outside those boundaries and is very different. In God's world or heaven, it is grander than beyond our human comprehension. The intensity of God's love is like a water atmosphere, so thick and wonderful. It meets the longing of our hearts for which we were made. The creativeness of God is without measure for us to conceive. Illustrating this would be like describing the pearly gates of heaven or the streets paved in gold and all sorts of precious gems. Heaven is the glory of God, an existence without sin. The glory of God is purity and holiness to the extreme. Without the ability for us to measure beyond what we can grasp, how are we to know unless God Himself reveals it to us? The best example that I can find in the Bible of one who has seen the Lord is in Isaiah 6:5:

> *"Woe to me!" I cried. "I am ruined! For I am a man of unclean lips, and I live among a people of unclean lips, and my eyes have seen the King, the Lord Almighty."*

Two Extremes

Evil is the first sin in heaven. It is Satan's sin, wanting to be as God Himself and convincing one third of the angels to follow him into rebellion against God Almighty. This was a very bad choice.

> *And the angels who did not keep their positions of authority but abandoned their proper dwelling—these he has kept in darkness, bound with everlasting chains for judgment on the great Day* (Jude 1:6).

It is well explained in Matthew Henry's Commentary (my paraphrase): Satan and his followers left their God-chosen and created positions. In God's desire, He created them perfect. In their rebellion they were saying they didn't like His choice for them and were dissatisfied, which was an insult to Father God. From heaven they were expelled from a life of opulence to the worst imaginable existence: damnation and a place created for their existence, hell.

There are two extremes: the wonders of heaven and the horrors of hell. In the middle of all of this is the earth and mankind. Heaven wants

that none should perish (John 3:16), and every person has the possi-
bility of being heaven-bound. Satan, knowing the beauty of heaven and
the fact that he will never be there again, hates all people and works to
keep every person from gaining entrance to heaven! I imagine a single-
line graph with zero at the center point. On the God side it ranges from
zero to one trillion, and on the evil side is zero to negative one trillion.
This is the range of experiences in the spiritual realm. Now the human
range on this same graph would be from a positive one hundred to a
negative one hundred. It falls far short of the total spiritual experience.
This is my word picture for you to grasp what happens beyond our
world into the battle for the souls of mankind.

New Creations

Now let's get back to God's plan for salvation. All of mankind has
free will, and we know that we will sin. We are born into original sin.
God needed to come up with a plan for our sins to be forgiven, and that
is where Jesus comes in. In heaven, a plan was forged—that Jesus would
come into the world, be born of a virgin woman, and become fully God
and fully man. He would be exposed to every possible temptation and
would not sin: something only God could do. On the cross, He gave up
His life as the Lamb of God because of God's own choice of actions to
be taken, even though they are very hard to grasp or imagine. Jesus suffered and died for the sins of mankind—for the remission of our sins. In
order to gain heaven after this life, we would need to be sinless. That is
something we humans just cannot do on our own. However, God extends the work Jesus came into the world to do for us. When we receive
it by our own by faith, His sinless life—His righteousness—is applied to
us.

- We believe that God is the Trinity—Father, Son, and Holy Spirit.
- Jesus was born of a virgin.
- Jesus was fully God and fully man.
- He lived a sinless life, being exposed to every kind of temptation
and yet didn't sin.

- He suffered and died on the cross for the forgiveness of my sins.
- He rose from the dead.
- We must understand that we are sinners.
- Our sins have caused Jesus pain and suffering.
- We must be willing to turn from the sins we are committing.
- He is Lord, He will lead our lives, and we will be willing to following Him (it will be for our good).

The above list is the seed of God for salvation. One of the best descriptions of God's plan for salvation comes in Romans 10:9-13:

> *If you declare with your mouth, "Jesus is Lord," and believe in your heart that God raised him from the dead, you will be saved. For it is with your heart that you believe and are justified, and it is with your mouth that you profess your faith and are saved. As Scripture says, "Anyone who believes in him will never be put to shame." For there is no difference between Jew and Gentile—the same Lord is Lord of all and richly blesses all who call on him, for, "Everyone who calls on the name of the Lord will be saved."*

Salvation

I know my main intent is to reach Christians and share my message from the Lord on inheriting the land. However, there may be many people who are reading this book who have not yet come to accept Jesus as Savior and Lord. I would like to connect with you as well. Being a volunteer for "Need Him Ministries," I take calls, sharing the Gospel with the callers and seekers. When a person wants to have Jesus in their lives, we pray together. So let's take a moment to pray now:

> Dear Father God, I thank You for Your Son, Jesus, and the work He did on the cross for me. I acknowledge to You that I am a sinner. I am sorry for the pain my sins have caused You. Pease forgive me. I now invite You, Jesus, to come into my heart and into my life, and I want to live for You. In Jesus' name we pray, amen.

If you have prayed that prayer for the first time, it is important to get connected to a church family to help nurture you and help you grow in your new spiritual life. Please read the Bible and absorb the living Word of God. Seek others who will take you under their wing and mentor you in your new walk with the Holy Spirit.

Second Blessing

This is the long way around to explaining the seeds coming to life that I sowed so many years ago. Let's look at the second blessing of being filled with the Holy Spirit. What is this all about anyway? I take the stand for the "filling of the Holy Spirit" because it has happened to me. I became involved with a group of Spirit-filled Christians. They led a study on this issue, hoping for others to receive the same blessing/filling. It was a six-week course meant for all new members and those seeking a deeper relationship with the Holy Spirit. On week five, mature Christians would come into the class for the purpose of laying on of hands with us in the class and turning our hearts toward Jesus, requesting that He baptize us with His Holy Spirit. I thought it was a single prayer, short and sweet. With six people around me, I was seated and they all entered their prayer closets and petitioned the Lord on my behalf. They had been praying for about five minutes when it happened.

I began to thank Jesus for His Holy Spirit and focus my thoughts and mind upon Him. A spiritual event happened, and a spiritual actuation began. I had no previous knowledge of it nor could I have conceived such a thing until this point. Water within my belly in the center of my spirit as its point of origin began to bubble up out of an opening and came forth! In an upward bubbling, I felt the context of the liquid flow. Like a drinking fountain that bubbles upward and then down to the bottom of the container, it flowed out of me. The temperature of the water was cool but not cold. It was filling my spirit quickly, and I felt it swirling within me. I was empty, then I was half-full and noticing that there were spiritual things in the water. Love! I felt such love as I had never felt before. Gifts—spiritual gifts were in the water, the birthing of services to come. I didn't know what to say or do, and before I knew it, I was full and could feel pressure pressing outward in all directions. I was

154

full of living water. What a great experience and the beginning of a new life, a power life in Jesus Christ (see Acts 19:4–7).

I have covered the essential points of a Christian's life: being born again and being filled with the Holy Spirit to empower your new spiritual birth. Both are extremely important for walking in the spiritual realm. This is groundwork for the next chapter on prayers.

One night, while lying in bed, I saw it: the life in the seeds I had sown previously and those newly sown! Being in the prophetic I know the importance of plowing the spiritual ground of communities. I had sown a seed of revival in my community. In a vision, the Lord showed me a church desperately seeking revival. Within days, I got connected to the church and a pastor. After several weeks of attending the Sunday services, I shared with the pastor that people I knew could aid him in his desire. In an earlier chapter I talked about Pastor Phil Corbett and the gift of reviving churches. Pastor Rob listened to my suggestion of having him come and hold services and took the idea to prayer. He contacted various people to get references for Pastor Phil. He called and asked him for sermons on CD. He wanted to listen and see if Pastor Phil might be a person whom he would consider sharing his pulpit with. Then they set a date to hold meetings. It was birthed.

Other seeds I have sown and have seen sprouting include the following: I shared with you the vision of churches inheriting the land, as in 2 Chronicles 7:14. I am now seeing this happening in Texas and the groundwork for it flowing beyond the state. I had a powerful vision of spiritual power flowing into a Hispanic community. Little did I know Hispanic communities in Chicago, in Anchorage, Alaska, and in other parts of the nation would all experience a birth of the Holy Spirit visiting in these communities! I watched economic tsunami waves crash in Chicago and devasting the entire Midwest region. The outcome has been people crying out to God for restoration and help (see Psalm 107) I receive calls from all over the nation from lukewarm Christians and coldhearted ones too. They have so much turmoil in their lives, they know that only God is the answer for them now. They are calling upon the Lord and He rushes to meet them and welcome them home.

Chapter 22

Let's Get Down to Prayer

I am an advocate for Christians coming into the spiritual realm of God. Stepping into the spiritual realm and beyond the boundaries of our world is very different from what we are used to. Just think of Paul having a godly dream of a man calling him to come to Macedonia. Philip was speaking with a man from Ethiopia one minute and then he was missing the next. How about the Day of Pentecost, when the Upper Room was filled with the presence of the Holy Spirit? They saw a tongue of fire come and rest upon each believer. A roaring wind swept across the city and came to rest with the apostles, and each person was filled with the Holy Spirit. It was personal to all of them.

Then there is the story of the sons of Sceva (see Acts 19:14–16). These men tried to move in the power of God and were not born again. They were not connected to the Holy Spirit but rather stood alone. They were outmatched by the evil spirit they were dealing with and lost. You must know who you are in Christ Jesus. You must yield to His authority in order to enjoy the fullness of dreams, visions, manifestations, and visitations from the Lord.

Because this book is about inheriting the land (spiritually) and being experiential Christians, I am not going to dig into the scriptural foundations of each prayer. That alone would take a couple of chapters to define. Some people might not believe in asking forgiveness for the sins of our fathers because they lived in times past. However, in my journey the Lord brought me to the following verse:

And it will be said: "Build up, build up, prepare the road! Remove the obstacles out of the way of my people" (Isaiah 57:14).

This is the prayer that I start with. My prayers are the result of being a student in my time spent with God. I begin by "removing the obstacles" of sins hindering His children's lives. It all starts with the sins of the fathers. So, let's begin:

Dear Father God,

I lift up to You those who are reading this prayer. I ask that You please cover them with the blood of Christ from the top of their heads to the bottom of their feet...that You would now station Your ministering and protecting angels around them with whatever ministry they need and whatever high ranking angels that are needed for their lives.

I ask, Father, that You would please forgive their forefathers for the sins they have committed that have caused You pain. We are sorry for that pain; please forgive them. In the name of Jesus, we break off every curse and stronghold and cancel all ground upon their life and cast them aside.

Let's now turn to the blessings.

Father,

I lift up the readers to You and ask that You would open a window to heaven over their lives. I ask that You would pour out Your provisions and Your blessings upon them without measure...that You, Lord, would fill their hearts with Your love.

I ask that You would release the elements of Your Holy Spirit into their lives. May You give them Your living water to flow into their lives and refresh their spirits. May the living water well up within them and flow out of them to all those whom they love and care about. Share with them the wind of Your Holy Spirit to bring Your changes into their lives and be a blessing to their families. Place their feet upon a path of Your design. Please release the power of Your Holy Spirit into them to create new things as only You can do.

May Your new life and gifts change the direction and course of their lives and be a blessing to them and their families. Father, may Your consuming fire enter their lives and remove all things that are not eternal. And may the fire of Your compassion burn within them and be contagious to all those around them.

Please allow your anointing oil to flow upon their heads and join them in a relationship with the Holy Spirit as You did to the apostles in the upper room on Pentecost. Open up a life of works and ministry for them, Lord.

Father, please place Your favor upon them. May Your favor go before them in all parts of their lives and be a blessing to them. It is in Jesus' name we pray. Amen!

Spiritual Cords/Connections

Let's progress to spiritual cords of the heart that are forged in relationships. David and Jonathan had a deep spiritual connection. Call it a cord forged in their life, and it was good. There are times when we forge a cord or a connection to ungodly people. It hinders us in negative ways. Soul ties and spiritual cords are controversial issues. There were times when I was hurting and didn't know why. I was seeking God desperately for the relief from the spiritual turmoil that I was in. The Lord led me to soul ties.

How did this introduction of this new soul tie dynamic enter my life? By the radio! During work, I was driving from one job to another to service the elevators. I turned on the radio that was already set to a local Hammond, Indiana, Christian station. It was the top of the hour and a program was just starting. The topic was "Generational Sins and Soul Ties." I had a huge tug to call in! Truly nervous, I dialed the number. Believe it or not, I got through and was the first caller.

It was a life-changing experience for my own life. The release of separating me from ungodly spiritual connections to people and cords forged by traumatic events in my early life was taking place as a result.

It was tangible. The separation process began, and I could tell something had happened. I started to use the principles that the pastor on the radio program shared with me. I incorporated those principles into my prayers. Things were different for me. I was freed from those unwanted intrusions in my life that the soul ties and cords brought. Now, I want to pray for you. Here is my prayer for breaking off the soul ties in your life. Let us pray:

Dear Father,
I bring before You the reader. I ask that if there is any ungodly soul ties or any traumatic events forging cords to other people, that in the name of Jesus Christ we gather all those cords together in a bundle. In the name of Jesus we now cut those cords and separate the reader from those ungodly soul ties. We ask that You make their spirit whole and of one piece where no evil thoughts can penetrate. In Jesus' name we pray. Amen!

This is a reminder for our continuous need to bring our sinfulness before God for forgiveness. We must set our hearts before God with a deep desire for Him to reveal our sins to us. Not all sins are visible to our minds. Some are hidden from our view. We seek Him to show us all of our sins, and we must be willing to turn away from them. Only at this point is when the change takes place. As individuals, corporately in the body of Christ, and in our nation as well, we need the outcome of repentance.

Our heartfelt actions get the attention of Father God. His compassion for us will release the provisions we need to heal our land.

Your Atmosphere

What in the world do I mean by "your atmosphere"? Your home, your ministry, and the places you work in—I consider these to make up your atmosphere. The next prayer is to set aside those places as a sanctuary for the Lord. I want you to see a transfer of ownership from the domain of Satan to the reign of God. Your inheritance as ministers and children of God is that He will bring healing to the land that you live in and minister in your atmosphere. So let's begin!

Dear Father God,

I bring before You the reader's home. I ask that whether it is a home, an apartment, or a rented room, whatever it is and wherever it is, You cover it with the blood of Jesus Christ. From the very top of the structure, completely down the outside, and everything inside is covered. Lord, I ask that it would go down to the foundation and out to the property lines. I ask that You would please forgive the sins that have taken place in this place or have taken place upon the ground that this dwelling is built upon. I am sorry for the pain that these sins have caused You; please forgive them.

Now Father, I ask that You station Your angels in this dwelling or home, that You station them inside the home and at the corners of the property lines. If there should be any demons in the home or on the property, please have Your angels escort them away right now. Let them be sent to wherever You tell them to go. Father, I would ask now that You release Your presence into this home and You would live with them in unity and peace. May Your love fill their home now in the name of Jesus Christ. Amen!

Another thing to consider is anointing your home. I may have ruffled several feathers by now, but I am a firm believer of setting aside your home by anointing it with oil, a symbol of the Holy Spirit. If you agree, symbolically anoint the entry points of the dwelling with oil and request God to set apart your home for Him.

Places of Ministry

What and where is your place of ministry? Is it in a church? Is it in a rented spot from a school or business? Wherever it may be, let's pray that God sets it apart for His presence to come and dwell with you.

Dear Father God,

I ask that You please cover this ministry with the blood of

Christ from the very top of the structure to the bottom down to the bottom, covering the foundation and flowing out to the property lines. Please cover everything outward and everything inward in the blood of Jesus. Please wash it clean and white as snow.

Father, please station Your angels inside the building and outside and on the corners of the property. I ask that if a high-ranking angel is needed to protect this ministry, that You would assign them to it now. Father, if any sins have taken place in this building or upon the ground on which it sits, we are sorry for these sins.

Father, we are sorry for the pain it has caused You; please forgive them. For all the ministries where there has been corporate sin, I ask that You would please forgive these sins and release unity. Lord, if there have been curses, spells, or voodoo, or occult activities toward this ministry and the staff, we break them off and cast them away right now in the name of Jesus. Now, if there should be any demons in the building or on the grounds, please have your angels escort them away and send them wherever You tell them to go. We anoint this structure with Your holy oil and set it apart for You. Please release Your presence into this ministry and make it an intersection of heaven and earth where people can come and experience Your presence.

I ask, Lord, that the church and ministry would inherit the land and all Your provisions to enrich and protect it. I ask that an abundant harvest would take place as You remove all the hindrances holding back the flow of Your grace and increase it to a deluge without limits. Let revival come to this church and ministry as You have for this new day. It is Your new move for our time in these final days.

Lord, if specific sins are needed to be repented of, reveal them to Your people so that they can be forgiven. In Jesus' name we pray. Amen!

Vision of January 20, 2006

As I am writing this chapter of the book, I continue to receive dreams from the Lord. I am seeing a disturbing decline in God's protection for our country. So I feel a need to again pray and decree the content of this vision.

Father,

In the name of Jesus Christ, I decree to Your daughters, the Church, those who are as little children before You:

I am to be the only inheritance the priests have. You are to give them no possession in Israel; I will be their possession (Ezekiel 44:28).

Lord, I decree Your inheritance to them right now. I decree and declare a transfer of the ownership of the land to them. Release all the provisions You have set aside for them. Release them right now and remove all barriers hindering the salvation of the lost and the fullness of Your habitation with them.

Father, I thank You for having compassion and healing their land. Thank You for coming and taking up residence with them and bringing liberty and freedom to their regions. In Jesus' name we pray. Amen!

Experiential Christians

The Lord has recently brought me to a place where I am able to step out and trust Him in sharing my experiential life. I have found many denominations accepting my relationship with the Holy Spirit. It is the desire of these churches to walk in the manifestations of the Holy Spirit and not to seek the gifts or manifestations. That would lead to spiritual problems. However, after we have a close relationship with the Holy Spirit, He releases gifts and visitations to us. It is because we believe this is available to us that we try to live with the "God outside the box" dynamic.

I am always cautious when it comes to encouraging people to enter the spiritual realm. We have prayed for a safe spiritual environment in our homes and around our lives. Now it is time to send out invitations for the Holy Spirit to come and visit us. Are you aware of the increase of the Holy Spirit? As darkness increases, so does the activity of God increase. Praise God! We have a promise in Joel that applies here:

"And afterward, I will pour out my Spirit on all people. Your sons and daughters will prophesy, your old men will dream dreams, your young men will see visions" (Joel 2:28).

Would you like to see into the spiritual realm as described in the scripture above and share it with others? Prophecy is being able to speak the heart of God to those around you. You are able to speak something out of nothing. That means that when the words flow over your lips, out loud, the message from God is now spoken into life here on earth. The "Word" comes alive! Coming alive, it is released and starts something new that wasn't there before. The new life will come through you for someone else as an encouragement or confirmation. This is what took place when I was at my sister Sue's house. It was new life provided by God through prophecy.

This new life started on a Saturday afternoon. My brother-in-law, Ed, and his wife, Sheila, were visiting from Florida with their fifth wheel. While I was sitting with Ed in front of the garage at Sue's house, I felt the Holy Spirit come upon me. It is not often that I move in the oral gift of prophecy. I felt the Holy Spirit's heart well up within my soul, and I found myself speaking words of a new life, a new legacy, and a new home for my sister.

Released in the spiritual realm were the words of God. Through prophecy, we saw unrestricted provisions that totally turned my sister's life upside down. It could be the subject of a book all by itself. Briefly stated, six months after I had prophesied, her town was devastated by a terrible storm and her house was flooded with two feet of water. Her home was legally condemned. We watched God drop one provision after another on this small eight-hundred-square-foot home. Eventually, she was able to replace the former home with a 1600-square-foot home. Its foundation now rests two feet above the flood plain. There is no doubt in our minds that God led her into a new legacy.

Dreams from God are wonderful in helping us to see what is behind the spiritual veil. They help us get an understanding of what is happening there. Then there are warning dreams. These are a call to prayer. Destiny dreams show you what the Lord's plans are for your life in the future. Many things may come to a child of God in His visits to him or her during the night. Visions are another story. There are at least four types of visions:

• You are fully awake, yet you are looking at something that is not there in your earthly field of vision.

• There is seeing something with your eyes closed, and you are fully awake. Open your eyes and it is gone, close your eyes and there it is. Be ready to pay attention to details.

• There are times when we are on the verge of falling asleep, and we will see something and wonder, *What was that?*

• And then there are the most powerful, trance visions like Peter had on the roof before he went to Cornelius's house. A trance vision holds you still until God can show you everything you are supposed to see and what is going to happen. It is set before you, as in life. These are scary at first. Once we learn to trust Him in the trance visions, they are not needed in the future. You are conditioned to receive them.

A great book to read on this subject of the Holy Spirit's activities in your life would be *Signs and Wonders*.[1] This is a diary of Maria Woodworth Etter's revival meetings as she and her people followed where the Lord led them. Now for the prayer:

Dear Father,

I lift up to You the readers and I ask that You would bless them with the promise found in Joel 2:28. Open up their eyes to the see visions from You, Lord. Open their ears to identify Your voice and hear from You. Bring them into a deeper relationship with the

Holy Spirit. Visit them during the night and allow them to interact with You and Your messengers. May they grow in their knowledge of You, align with the Scripture for validation, and move from glory to glory. In Jesus' name we pray. Amen!

This is the advice that I give when I am encouraging a person to seek an experiential relationship with the Holy Spirit. When you get ready to fall asleep and your head is on the pillow, invite the Holy Spirit to come visit you during the night. Be expectant! When you first experience Him in a supernatural way, it is often different and scary. You can then step back and ask Him to verify your experience with the Scriptures. Many times the Lord will prepare me, days in advance, that there is going to be a visitation and to expect it, to yield to it. This has been a great help to me even today. It has been many years since I started down this road. Jesus is gentle and never pushy.

Closing Spiritual Doors

I have found it a good practice to find and locate sin in my life. Why? Where sin exists, there is an open door for evil to attack. A very good recourse for seeing and locating sin in our lives from our past is a book called *The Bondage Breaker*.[2] The reason that I like this book is that it helps to pinpoint problem areas in your life and heritage. The author has prayer suggestions to close the doors that these sins have opened up in your life. It doesn't matter if the sins were committed by your actions or those who came before you. It is important to discern where your experiences are coming from: God or evil.

What words of wisdom can I pass on to you as you enter the spiritual realm of God? Let me try. Once I was filled with the Holy Spirit, my feet were placed upon a path that I felt compelled to follow. At first, I ran from God. How foolish was that? Then I woke up and realized I had to succumb to the pressure and follow Him. I began to pray so that I could be used by Him in spiritual contexts. I just don't know why I prayed for that. It was laid upon my heart and I followed like a child. I prayed for two years before I could see something different begin to happen. At first, I was so shaken by my experience that I stepped back. God then showed me it was really Him and to follow. It took a while, but again I yielded and was shown things I could have not known on my own. Everything started to fall into place, baby steps at a time! Little growth took place in time, and my trust in Him grew. It can happen with you, as well!

It is ultimately important to spend one-on-one time with the Holy Spirit each day. It is your heaven-and-earth connection that will change your spiritual life forever. Do you like the Bible stories of Jacobs's life, the son of Isaac? My point in his life is this—God said to Jacob in a dream: "I am with you and will watch over you wherever you go" (Genesis 28:15). Hebrews 11 is the chapter on the heroes of faith. Because they believed in God and experienced Him in their journey of faith, they changed the world around them. We too have the same opportunity to experience God in this type of relationship. Know beyond a shadow of doubt that God is with you as your hero of faith. Know Him just like Jacob knew Him! You can know God this intimately.

However, as it is written: "What no eye has seen, what no ear has heard, and what no human mind has conceived" the things God has prepared for those who love Him—these are the things God has revealed to us by his Spirit (1 Corinthians 2:9–10).

Chapter 23

Go and Sin No More

In the previous chapter, we prayed prayers to close doors to evil's access to your life. I want to share with you two Scriptures. First:

And he that was healed wist not who it was: for Jesus had conveyed himself away, a multitude being in that place. Afterward Jesus findeth him in the temple, and said unto him, Behold, thou art made whole: sin no more, lest a worse thing come unto thee. The man departed, and told the Jews that it was Jesus, which had made him whole (John 5:13–15 KJV).

And the second Scripture is John 8:10–12 (KJV):

When Jesus had raised Himself up and saw no one but the woman, He said to her, "Woman, where are those accusers of yours? Has no one condemned you?" She said, "No one, Lord." And Jesus said to her, "Neither do I condemn you; go and sin no more." Then Jesus spoke to them again, saying, "I am the light of the world. He who follows Me shall not walk in darkness, but have the light of life."

Our heart is the doorway into the spiritual realm. When we sin, we open ourselves to evil and all the entanglements connected to that type of sin and its stronghold upon us. We can also choose to open our hearts to the ways of God and all the blessings they bring to our lives and all those in our lives. If you have prayed the prayers in the previous chapter, you have closed the doors to evil that may have been open in your life. We closed doors that others had opened who came before us. All the doors need to stay closed!

A Tale of Two People

Let me give you a little information on how the phone ministry works since you may not be familiar with it. I am always amazed at how God connects the right people together. He matches the caller's needs with the volunteer who has the right gift to meet the caller's needs. I am using the following two tales because they easily explain my point. They are rather dramatic but they work.

This first tale is a story about Sara. I met Sara by phone when she called the Need Him Ministries' phone number. Sara lives in Kingman, Arizona. Her needs were not the normal requests. She lived in an apartment building and was having spiritual problems. Need Him Ministries is an evangelistic ministry for the purpose of sharing the Gospel of Jesus Christ in hopes of bringing people into a personal relationship with Jesus. I would share with callers God's plan of salvation. Then I would pray with them to receive Him as Lord and Savior. With each caller, the first thing I want to understand is how much they know of the Christian faith and God's plan for their salvation from their sins. Sometimes the caller is already a Christian and is looking for prayer or spiritual advice. Today, there were not many calls coming in and I had the time to address Sara's problem.

She began to tell me that she was no longer sleeping in her bedroom because of the terrible nightmares she was having in that room. She had to sleep on the couch. Neither Sara, nor her daughter wanted to go in the bedroom because of how uneasy they felt there. Once I understood her situation, we prayed together. I was using the prayers from the previous chapter. Immediately, the atmosphere of her apartment changed. She moved into the bedroom while still talking to me and lay down on the bed. Her daughter happened to walk by the doorway and asked her what she was doing in there. It had turned from uneasy feelings to peaceful feelings. God now occupied her home!

168

I hadn't logged in to the ministry for three weeks. On Saturday afternoon, my third call of the day was Sara! Now really, what are the chances of that happening apart from God? There are 447 volunteers at this time. Our amazing God connected the two of us together again. Sara was glad I answered, since I knew her story, and she told me the evil presence was back. I started to ask her questions about what was happening in her life and within a few minutes I understood the problem. She had unwittingly opened the door to sin and the evil was back. I don't think the type of sin is important here. But she had stepped outside her protective boundaries. Sara, in her ignorance of Scripture, sinned and reopened the door. This is why Jesus told His people, "Go and sin no more." Once I explained it to her, she said, "I am going to sit down and read the Bible so this doesn't happen again!"

The second story concerns dreams. I do dream mentoring with others by e-mail. Someone suggested that Bill should contact me. As a new Christian, his bigger-than-life dreams were new to him. He asked for help. For more than twenty-five years I have been learning to understand the dreams God blesses me with. Once I receive a dream or vision from the Lord, I seek Him for its meaning. I have two helpful books that I refer to: *The Prophets' Dictionary*[1] and *Understanding the Dreams You Dream.*[2] With these two resources, I usually come within 60 percent of knowing the message hidden within the dream. Personal knowledge and experiences also play a big part of the symbolism held with the dreams and visions we receive.

Now back to Bill. He was a new believer and was having terrible nightmares. He didn't like to go to sleep at night. He wrote out his dreams for me and I helped him along the way. I prayed with him, using the prayers in the previous chapter. The atmosphere of his home changed, and he began sleeping a full eight hours. This was something he hadn't enjoyed for some time. However, within two weeks, the sense of evil was back. He sought the Lord for help. And, very clearly, he got the rhema word conveying to him that it was the result of opening the door to evil through his sin.

Hedge of Protection

I am sure you have heard the expression hedge of protection somewhere along the way during your Christian growth. It has been my experience that the Lord has protective boundaries around our lives. However, if I should go outside of those boundaries, I am fair game for the enemy to attack. I pray for the Lord to show me how I stepped outside of my protection and ask Him to forgive me and again the hedge is returned.

Most people know what Revelation 3:20 says. However, not many of us know the verse that precedes it:

"As many as I love, I rebuke and chasten. Therefore be zealous and repent" (Revelation 3:19).

Our loving God will allow us to experience uncomfortable things for the purpose of helping us to grow. This growth comes with new knowledge of how the Scriptures work and how they are applied to our lives. I demonstrated this concept using the tale of two people. They were getting hands-on experience from the Lord's chastening. They needed to stay within biblical guidelines for living a Christian life. I have experienced this chastening and have found it to be a wonderful setup for:

"Here I am! I stand at the door and knock. If anyone hears my voice and opens the door, I will come in and eat with that person, and they with me" (Revelation 3:20).

Hopefully, after we have been chastised, we will make some changes. What heart isn't ready to hear the knock on the door? Our hearts will welcome that knock with new reception and enthusiasm.

This thought ties in with the parable in Matthew 25. There were ten virgins. Only five wise virgins were waiting for the bridegroom with extra oil for their lamps, just in case they had to wait longer than expected. The extra oil represents our relationship with the Holy Spirit. If ever we need to have an extra oil relationship with Him it is now! Take a look around and be observant of the point in time we are now in as it relates to the Church and world history.

Sometimes, our habits are hard to break. Temptation and falling into sin reopens the door to evil attacks. We can feel the effects of our choices. There is nothing like a little struggle and pain to motivate me to change.

With evil on the outside of your door, you are now off and running. It is time to experience God in a new and wonderful way. There are times we experience attacks from the enemy, through spiritual warfare, for whatever reason. This whole chapter is about maintaining and closing the doors to evil. This could be a first for you: "Go and sin no more!"

Chapter 24

Amos

There has definitely been a progression in my spiritual growth. One step at a time leads me to another adventure, a puzzle to solve, new knowledge, and learning a new lesson. I really do enjoy the learning part, but the growth and change is another matter. The internal work on self is very hard and requires obedience to follow the Holy Spirit. I sometimes become a straggler in my journey. The Lord is generally patient with me. There are other times when He gets behind me to lend a push.

In the first half of the journey, I walk slowly, looking at all the possible dangers along the way. I straggle behind and the Lord graciously calls to me to pick up the pace. Then I hit the halfway mark. He shows me the marker and shazam, I am high-stepping it out of the valley. By the time I can see the way out, I am exhausted, pressed, stretched, and changed. I am closer to the man I need to be for God's planned ministry for my life.

I previously shared with you the release of my vision of 2006 at the pastor's conference in Gonzales. Relating to that day, I had just finished speaking, and I sat down and enjoyed the next part of the program. In the evening service, during the ushering in of the presence of God, I sat back into my seat, picked up my Bible, and it fell open to the first page of the book of Amos. Then it started. The book of Amos continually kept coming in front of me in many ways. For six months I was determined it was not a message. The voice of the Holy Spirit was not speaking to me. Have you ever read the book of Amos? What in the world would God have for me to see in the book of Amos? But I yielded to Him and read it again and again. Seven times I read this small book of the Bible. I began to see the message held within and how the Lord wanted it to be applied to our day, in our country.

Digging deeper I gravitated to my "fallback teacher": *Matthew Henry's Commentaries.*[1] He breaks down the Scriptures in ways that I can't imagine. I began to see the lines of printed text differently. I began to see new knowledge that was held within each line that I didn't see before. It centralized the message about repentance that you read about earlier.

Amos is from the Hebrew and means "to be burdened, troubled." I was becoming troubled by the correlation regarding the content held in the book of Amos and the current spiritual position of the United States of America. Who is straining to remember the content in the book of Amos? I love God. His ways are higher than our ways. His thoughts are higher than our thoughts. The established, organized, traditional religion had moved so far away from God's original design that the leaders of Judaism were as much the problem as the people were. It looked like this word picture: 5 percent spiritual life and 95 percent acceptance of fashionable sins of the day. They had become desensitized to the sins of their day!

Did God choose one of His big gun people, high in their spiritual ranks, to set them straight? Nope! He didn't even use a middle man holding a religious position in their day. He went to the lowest rung on the ladder, a person who was so unlikely it was going to be totally out of character for him to challenge a nation in sin. Amos was a shepherd who lived in the open plains with the herds. What did he know of challenging the system filled with the status-quo leaders?

God led him to reveal a plan. He was to confront human nature, the I-am-living-a-better-spiritual-life-than-the-other-guy mentality. That was how Amos started. He called out the sins of the neighboring country and tribes. His countrymen wholeheartedly agreed with him, they were sinners (heathens). Then Amos focused on the sins of Israel. One by one he spoke of their sins and aired them before the leaders, the people, and whoever would listen. In all honesty, they thought they were living a better life than their heathen neighbors. In reality, there wasn't much difference in their spiritual walk and the sins they were committing in relationship to all the countries around them. They had become calloused and blinded and no longer in touch with their fallen spiritual nature.

The defining moment, the sledgehammer to their glass rationalization, was when he told them their grave sin. They had known the true and living God! There was no excuse for them. They had the light of the knowledge of God and they had forsaken Him. In their sins the light of God's spiritual viability went out, and they practiced a lifeless religion still thinking they were better than the other guy, but it was not so.

Why did God send Amos onto the scene to challenge Israel? They were on a collision course with disaster! Amos was the man to save the day and show them the errors of their ways. Right there, right then, was when the destiny of Israel was held in the balance. Did they see their God? Were they giving Amos's witness of God's pending judgment and His advent credence in the critical fork in the road ahead of them? Would they discount Amos' premise as to the depth of their sins and offensiveness to God? Would they continue in the comfort of their present-day life and stay in denial? Or would they see that continuing to accept the sins of the day would lead their entire nation into the loss of their freedom and wealth?

What was the most important means to save this nation? It was contained in their human hearts! Sin is a spiritual act; the human emotional heart functions in the spiritual realm. To keep their freedom, Israel needed to repent of their sins. Repentance is an emotional heart issue empowered by the grace of God to activate. This activation only happens when humans seek Him.

God Does It

Let me define this a little more. In the times I have felt the spiritual function of repentance, God's grace touched my heart and folded back the protective walls. A portion of my emotional heart was exposed for me to feel. I saw my sins for what they were—transgression against a holy God. I knew the pain associated with those sins and how it caused God pain. In a rush I felt how truly sorry I was for hurting Jesus. I would not have seen the effect of sin if it weren't for the grace and the spiritual life held in its contents of grace. A nasty ability we have is to be able to rationalize and justify our actions even if they are blatant sins. We just make them okay in our minds and push them aside and keep on sinning. Finally, our rebellion, transgression, and the iniquity of our hearts tip the scales. Our sins must be atoned for one way or the other. We must humble ourselves before God. We must seek His grace and be vulnerable to look at the depravity of our sins and repent. Can we really shake our fist at God and believe that consequences are not going to happen?

Pastor Phil came to my church last weekend and held four services. He helped to usher in revival. In the first three services, the Holy Spirit had a plan. In His grace and within the atmosphere of the Holy Spirit, those of us with abuse and inner trauma issues could feel His grace stirring things up on the inside. The reaction of many was to run! Yes, people got up and paced the floor. They went to the back and moved farther away. Were they reducing the inner feelings that they had been detached from?

Why? It is overwhelming to deal with all the pain and trauma that we hold inside. Praise God, the people stuck it out. Service after service the Holy Spirit came upon various people. He worked on bringing up the issues and pain. When it was done and over, they were new people and praised God with renewed vigor and worship. God cleaned and healed them from the inside out.

Is the presence of God sought after anymore? When He shows up in a church service, all types of things happen—healings, salvations, deliverance. The love of God saturates our souls, and we long to linger in the house of the Lord. An all-important event is when God's children are brought into the holy of holies during a church service. Have you heard of this event before? Have you experienced this before? Twice the Lord brought me into a place of such holiness, and it changed me forever.

Humans think that we are really not bad people. On a human level you may be right. I had to remind myself that God, the Trinity, and of all His angels are not humans! They don't think like we do, nor live as we do.

When I had my life-changing experience, I can best describe it like I popped into a spiritual place even though I was still standing in church. My spirit had popped into the holy of holies. Instantly I knew the holiness of God was beyond our human understanding, and there was no scale to register it. The price Jesus paid for our sins is something that no human being could ever pay. Only God Himself could pay the price, and that is why Jesus came. There were many other things that happened in that experience that do not apply here.

Trouble starts when we grow comfortable with sin. We lose the perspective of the holiness of God. We can only come into His holy place by seeking Him and humbling ourselves before Him.

How can humans get to that holy place if our sins and pain levels are so high we run from the presence of God when He arrives? How do we come into repentance when we think our sins really aren't that bad and don't offend God very much?

Either we do the work God requires and repent of our sins or our blessings will be withdrawn by God and we lose our freedom and liberty. It is going to be work one way or the other.

During Amos's day, there was the story of Eli the high priest. The people's hearts were so filled with sins that the spiritual life of a nation had grown cold and lifeless. There was a city in the Bible that was challenged to confront their sins or lose their way of life: Nineveh! God had given them forty days to make up their minds, and that is exactly what they did. They listened and gained the favor of God. They continued on with life and a new heart toward God. I am not sure that the chronological order is correct here, but the message and outcome are. In Amos' day, the leading class—the high priest and the kings—walked in decades of prosperity and got too big for their britches. Father God saw that they needed a correction.

This morning I was reading from the *Zondervan NIV Study Bible*. I found something that is worth sharing with you. It includes the opening comment paragraphs at the beginning of the book of Amos. When you read it, keep in mind a reflection of our country at our current time.

Dates and Historical Situation

According to the first verse, Amos prophesied during the reign of Uzziah over Judah (793-753 B.C.) and Jeroboam II over Israel (793-753 B.C.). The main part of his ministry was probably carried out c.760-750. Both kingdoms were enjoying great prosperity and had reached new political and military heights. It was also a time of idolatry, extravagant indulgence in luxurious living, immorality, corruption of judicial procedures, and oppression of the poor. As a consequence, God would soon bring about an Assyrian captivity of the northern kingdom (722-721).

Israel at the time was politically secure and spiritually smug. About 40 years earlier, at the end of his ministry, Elisha had prophesied the resurgence of Israel's power, and more recently Jonah had prophesied her restoration to a glory not known since the days of Solomon. The nation felt sure, therefore, that she was in God's good graces. But prosperity increased Israel's religious and moral corruption. God's past punishments for unfaithfulness were forgotten, and his patience was at an end—which he sent Amos to announce.

With Amos, the message of the prophets began to be preserved in permanent form, being brought together in books that would accompany Israel through the coming debacle and beyond.

Organized Religion

In my thoughts I have pondered the question: Has organized religion in Christianity become a part of our current-day problem? From my perspective, being a blue collar worker in the business world's labor force limits my inroads into influencing Christian denominations. Why? I didn't come from within the system with all the education required to know the Bible and historical studies. I have tried to reach the clergy placed before me to share with them my experiential Christian walk. I was dismissed as not being credible. I am not knocking the leadership, but I have had to learn and try alternate approaches as God leads me. It is getting more serious for us here in the United States. The time is getting short in several ways. I am determined to be an influence for God as He opens the doors.

What is your question hanging in the air? "Well, Tom, did you ever think about entering the ministry and going to Bible school?" The answer is yes! At three different points in my life, I took the steps to enter school and the doors were not open. On my last attempt, I registered and received my first books to start a class. For two weeks I dove into the material and tried to get this seasoned brain to retain new information. Then—"Bam!" God literally turned my life upside down and I was fighting for survival. The last thing on my mind was finishing the course. By the time I was out of this trial, I gave up on the idea. Even though I am unschooled, the Lord is opening up doors for me to speak. Praise God. I know this is a tad confusing, and when you are walking with the Holy Spirit, it is a "learn as you go" kind of thing. The pivotal time was when I believed that God was calling me and going to use me for something. I entered a blind-man's-bluff game in the spiritual world that we don't see with human eyes nor hear with our human ears. I was learning to tune in to the art of using our spiritual eyes and ears.

What Role Do I Play?

Let me focus my train of thought here. Referencing my vision for my daughter's inheritance, I saw myself signing legal papers that would guard their inheritance. It is now six years down the road, and I am still gleaning knowledge from that vision. There is no doubt that small churches have been open to me speaking. The doorway for me is co-laboring with Pastor Phil. He has extended his good name in pastors' circles and encouraged them to include me in some of his meetings. It is obvious that small churches do not have many financial resources. In that atmosphere, they often cry out to God. It is their desire to have a breakthrough in the spiritual realm, and the heavens opened. That is just what we need in our day. They welcome the help. Pastors know the church's ministry is not a lone-ranger type of ministry. It is a fivefold ministry, and we need each department to achieve a vibrant spiritual life in Jesus Christ. I must note that there are also small churches that are not interested.

Now I have gained some practical experience speaking in small churches. The doors that are open are the ones where their hearts are humbled before God as little children. There are great pressures put on the backs of pastors. Financially it can be a real strain. Sometimes there is hardly enough money coming in to pay the bills of the ministry alone. This means that the pastors and their wives often need to work other part- or full-time job to support their basic needs.

In the depth of pain and suffering, God shows up and the miracles begin to happen. In contrast, the larger churches have many resources and most often work within the organized system (my perspective). I have yet to see a door open within a large church, but hopefully, that day is coming.

What door do we need to take to be in the right fork of the road? It can be found in: Amos 5:4, "This is what the Lord says to Israel, Seek me and live."

Seeking God is the first step of humbling our human hearts toward Him. When the grace touches your heart and the stirring of pains and trauma start to surface, don't run; press in! When the knowledge and sight of the filthiness of your own sin is before you and it is hard to look at, press in! It can happen in your church service, home, or anywhere that you least expect it. Either way, seek God! Press in!

What Will You Do?

Pastor Phil gave a message that asked the question, what will you do in your hour of visitation from the Lord? I see an increase of the spiritual flow of the Holy Spirit happening. It is an awaking of the hot spots of God's activity. There is the flow of spiritual life, and His presence is breaking out. It is going to cross your path. You may even seek those hot spots out like people did by going to places like Pensacola, Florida, for a revival meeting. It will be a multidenominational move of God. What will you choose to do when you enter His presence?

I am not one to tell people a course of action they are to take. However, when it comes to repentance, it is a win-win event. I am dead serious when I say that in the United States of America we are at a crossroads. We are in the same position that Israel was in during the time of the book of Amos. I believe that there is time. But the day might come when we will lose our freedom, just as Israel did. It can be avoided! One heart at a time, things can change. You will remember that 2 Chronicles 7:14 said that if we humble ourselves before God He will heal our land.

Now I am going to tell you why it is of extreme importance!

Chapter 25

Captivity

In December 2009, I sent off an e-mail to Pastor Phil. Just like many of the stories and events you have already read in the previous chapters, I had a dream and it held an assignment. I didn't understand it at first, but the marvelous information held within the dream fit a couple whom Pastor Phil knew. He then connected me with Pastor Gerome and his wife, Portia. There were details in the dream only this couple could recognize. It held seven parts. I was shown their current activities, past locations where they had lived, their two sons, and their desire for a move of God. Until Pastor Phil connected us together, I had been stuck. I didn't know whom the dream was for. There was a key piece of the dream that pointed Pastor Phil to the couple—the woman in the dream had a Native American bloodline.

Introductions were made through e-mails, and the dilemma they were in began to unfold. Portia is a woman of many words. I received e-mails that were filled with all kinds of details that I needed to understand. Once I could see where the flow of divine order was being interrupted, I could give advice and assist with prayers. It was a tangled mess. The part that really mattered was that Portia and her husband, Gerome, were crying out to God from their hearts. Portia, a pastor's wife, led a small prayer group. In one of the scenes in the dream I saw five ladies standing in a circle of prayer pleading with Father God to help them. God heard their cries and gave me their assignment.

Once I had a strong leading from the Lord, I wrote a plan to help change the spiritual atmosphere they were living in and labeled it "Step 1." In the next step I wrote up a prayer for their need. You've already read a good portion of the prayer.

Have you ever had deep pains and troubles that have run for a long period of time? I have. When this happens in your life, you are about ready to try anything God brings across your path. Pastor Gerome and Portia were in that place in their lives.

Portia did Step 1 and then read the prayer before retiring for the night. While she was sleeping, a spiritual presence came on her with power and centralized around her hip. The power that came upon her felt like electricity without the pain that you would have by touching a live wire. She knew something different had happened. After the Holy Spirit had withdrawn, she lay there praying and hoping. In the morning, she knew with every step she took the pain in her hip was gone. For years she had struggled with the pain and the difficulties it added to her life. The timing couldn't have been better. Portia had a scheduled doctor's appointment and upon examination the doctor confirmed she had been healed of her hip problem. Portia, filled with joy, is now proclaiming Jesus' healing power, as she dances her way through the day.

Connections to Next Adventure

I am amazed at the tapestry of God's hand! On my end, it started with a dream from God. Praying that He would bring me to the right people, I took my first step, to ask Pastor Phil if he could see anything in the dream. He then led me to Portia and Pastor Gerome. It so happened this couple were very good friends with Pastor Jim and Anita. I had met them at the pastors' conference in Gonzales, Texas, in October. Upon hearing of the healing of Portia, Pastor Jim opened the door for Pastor Phil and me. We traveled to Terrell, Texas, and held meetings the first week in February 2010. I flew in on Saturday, the sixth of February. Pastor Phil would drive from his home and meet us on Sunday evening.

On Sunday morning I would speak at Pastor Jim's church in Terrell, Texas. Pastor Phil would hold a revival meeting on Sunday night in

Elmo, Texas. On Monday morning I would share a teaching at Pastor Gerome's location in Elmo, Texas, and Pastor Phil would hold a meeting in the evening.

My flight into Dallas, Texas, was a first for me. The plane was to land about 1 p.m. I would pick up my rental car and drive east to the hotel that Pastor Jim had reserved for us. It was on the eastern side of Terrell, closest to his home and church. I have relied on driving directions before and I was really glad I had Rachel, my portable GPS system. I plugged in the address of the hotel and set out following the prompts given by Rachel in her feminine voice. "Be prepared to turn in two miles." Rachel told me she got dizzy upon reaching downtown Dallas. There are four intersecting expressways that make a square around downtown Dallas. From one interchange to another, there was a short span. The GPS didn't know what to tell me, so I was on my own. Focused and determined, I stayed on course. I have this quirkiness: I don't like to backtrack or lose time along the way. Once on the east side of Dallas, Rachel regained her composure and stopped telling me to make an immediate U-turn. When we were both on the same page, and it was clear sailing from there.

Once I was settled in at the hotel, I got a phone call from Jim and we set a time for him to pick me up. He wanted me to see the church. He wanted us to have a chance to talk before things got busy. The church was about five miles from the hotel, deep in the country. I'm glad that he showed me the way because I don't know if Rachel could have gotten me there.

His church is right next to his home on acres of his property. The church building had a crawl space below, and it was rectangular. Entering the main door we stepped into a kitchenette area, and Pastor Jim made some coffee. On the other end was Jim's office, our destination. It was small and functional. His desk was on the back wall, and a love seat was positioned opposite the desk on the inner wall. There was a set of attached bookshelves on the outer wall of this room. As we walked into his office he gestured for me to take his desk chair. I felt that he was honoring me. He sat on the love seat and got comfortable.

What a pleasure it was for me to talk with this man. His depth of spiritual things was awesome. His love for the Word of God was very clear to me. We shared stories of spiritual battles in the Lord. We then moved on to experiences in the spiritual realm and the knowledge it brings. We also talked about his mechanical abilities and common sense when it came to practical applications. He was very successful in the manufacturing world. Jim pastored part-time and worked full-time as many small church pastors need to do. At the two-hour mark of our conversation, things really got exciting.

Off the top shelf, a book was catapulted into the air and fell between our feet. He looked at me, I looked at him, and I said, "Jim, if this had happened to anyone else, they would be running for the door right now." I went on to say, "I think we were just given a message." Leaning over, I picked up the book to see the cover. What in the world was I going to do with this? The title of the book was The Declaration of Independence and the Constitutions of the United States of America, courtesy of Dr. D. James Kennedy and Coral Ridge Ministries.

Sitting there, stunned, not sure what to do or make of it, I handed him the book. He looked at it and handed it back to me to set on his desk. We went back to talking, but it wasn't the same as before. There seemed to be a sense of mystery and knowing that we were not alone, and that feeling overshadowed us. Before long it was ten o'clock and Jim drove me back to the hotel. What went on at the meetings that Pastor Phil and I held is not the focus here. I won't go into details about that. What is important is what took place after I arrived home that changed things.

Lord, Don't Let It Happen

At home I had the following dream: I was standing at attention with my controller (the person of ultimate authority over my life) on my right side. My co-laborer was on the other side of the female controller. We are working as caretakers for an elitist in their home. The job at hand is the operations of running a dinner to feed the elitists. Suddenly, my controller starts barking orders, and without hesitation we jump into a frenzied activity to please our master. Our task took us into the kitchen and we were alone. While we were both at the sink, I risked speaking to my partner and you could see the fear upon his face. If we were caught talking, severe punishment would be inflicted on us. Driven by my desire to escape and gain my freedom, as quietly as possible I spoke about plans to escape. He would hear none of it. Every waking moment of my internment I thought of only one thing: freedom.

The controller came back into the kitchen, and we busied ourselves with the work of cleaning up after dinner. Again when we were alone, I spoke of escape. It is all I lived for—I had no rights, I was not free, and I was under the control of a ruling class. I had lost everything that I had ever worked for. My family, home, career, finances are all gone. The only reason I was alive was because I could work. I was at the ruling classes' beck and call. That is all I was allowed to do. The atmosphere was one of intense fear. To displease my master would mean sudden punishment and often death. The will to survive stirred within me. The joy of being a free man cried to me again. I kept running thoughts through my mind: How can I gain my freedom? In the pit of my stomach I detested my captors. They had all the power concerning my life. At any moment it could all end. I must do as they say if I was ever going to have any hope of being free again.

In Shock

Startled awake, my emotions were intense, and I felt as if I had just lived the experience I dreamed about. My heart was pounding; the fear of being held captive was a sickening pit in my stomach. I had a taste of what it is to be a prisoner, not by breaking the law, but by takeover.

Citizens across America had lost their freedom, and we were now a huge, controlled labor force for a ruling class. This was the experience I had just had in this more than real dream! I didn't know what to make of this; it was so real. Within minutes I begin to pour out my heart to God to have mercy on America. For several hours I lay there and prayed. My very freedom could be at stake. The Church had fallen asleep and now I was in an intercessor's role for the nation. Tears streamed down my eyes for several hours. I am at a loss to tell you how terrible the experience was and how deeply it touched my life. For days I thought about the experience. I sought God and prayed for understanding.

Again, within days, I was caught up in a dream. I was standing outside and again I must stand at attention. I was on a landing of stairs to a level change. There were twenty stairs leading upward and to the right. There were six stairs leading down to the ground. A road was just at the base of the stairs, and there were military vehicles passing by from an occupying force. America had been invaded. Soldiers with assault weapons were standing nearby. Their guns were ready. I watched as the transport vehicles passed in a steady stream. I could not speak. I was to stand there until I was ordered to move. The soldiers' uniforms are green. They do not speak English, and it is toward the end of the day. Nighttime was approaching when I awoke. My heart was pounding and I was feeling sick to my stomach with the experienced fear.

Lying in bed, I wondered, *Lord, what in the world is going on?* I again started to pray and plead for mercy upon America. I asked for forgiveness of the sins our country was committing. I pleaded with the Lord not to allow this to happen to us. Hours went by, and I hadn't even noticed I was so into speaking with God. Sheer fear rushed through my body and mind as I reflected on my dream experience. We had lost it all. Everything that was mine, everything the citizens of America owned, was now theirs. We lost it all.

Third Dream

Within days, I was caught up in another dream. I was working in a theater for the elitist entertainment. I ran the dreary tasks of the upkeep of the organization—things needed be cleaned; bills needed to be passed out' people need to be seated. My controller was never far away. This was forced labor—I had no choice in the matter. My life was now theirs to do with as they please. Escape was weighing in on my every thought. But could do I pull it off? I must escape at all costs. I woke up with my heart pounding and I entered into another intercession for our nation. By now you get the picture.

I had one more dream that started as I was in a great open area. Green grass stretched across the rolling hills in a place I cannot identify. There was a group of us, men and women frantically trying to make decisions on which way to go. However, without knowing our location, we were guessing on the best way to gain our freedom. We had somehow escaped. We had heard of a border—our captives evidently did not have control over all of America. If we could make our way past the border we would be free again. My wife and I, along with my best friend of forty years and his wife, all forged a plan. We will split up and the first ones out will get a vehicle and wait for the other guys before leaving our captors behind. Then we would all drive deep into the land of freedom again to live life as we have known it before.

After embracing each other, we set off walking. We were making our way on the edges of shadows and tree lines. We tried to conceal our bodies from the military ruling class. Tired beyond belief, we were driven to escape. The fear of punishment and most likely death was what motivated us to forge ahead. To our surprise, my wife and I found the way to the border. It happened to be a place not guarded by the military. Quickly we crossed over and immediately we had a minivan and the keys were in it, and it started. I had more fear now that I was free than when I was striving to gain it. Sitting in the car, our minds were racing to make a fast decision. What do we do now? We have made a promise to wait for my lifelong friend and his wife. Looking into the face of my wife the "what ifs" ran through my mind. Is my friend going to even make it out? Did he take the same route that would lead him to this spot? Have they been lost or recaptured? What do I do? Wait?

Seconds passed as if they were hours. Our fear was rising unabated. Our captors didn't play by the rules. They would have no problem with coming into the free land and forcing us to go back with them into captivity. We had no one here who would protect us if they did indeed come across after us. We were waiting but we were on our own. In my mind, I knew there was no way to know if they were coming. I started up the minivan and drove away.

I was that desperate, I was dying inside myself, and I just abandoned my friends. The heartfelt emotions of leaving them behind were tearing away at me. I was too afraid of losing our freedom again. I couldn't be sure that they were really coming to this spot in their escape. In my heartbroken expressions, gut-wrenching feelings, I left them. Tears streaming down my face, I headed into freedom, but I was less free now.

I had broken a promise I shouldn't have made. You will make all kinds of deals to aid you in your quest for freedom. I made mine. Foolish or not, I wanted him to be there for me if he got out first. We had made flawed plans. Even though this happened, my life was never going to be the same. I woke up devastated by what had just transpired in this dream. When I tell this dream to others, it is hard for me. I still break down and cry when touching those emotions.

What can I say, folks? I have had more than seventy of these dreams. I have never had more than three dreams on the same issue before. But I have had more than seventy of these same kind of dreams. In this last Memorial Day's dream, I did escape. I left with no shirt on my back. I was given one on the way to freedom. I was that desperate.

I Got It Now

Let me paint you a word picture. Any size boat displaces water to be buoyant and float. In America, reflecting on the message Amos gave us, holiness is needed for God to release provisions to keep us safe. Without a season of repentance, we will lose our freedom. Then, in the throes of captivity, we will be humbled. We will be in a place to repent. It will be too late! We will go down as a nation.

When I saw the book in Jim's office fly off the top shelf, it told me, with the combination of the dreams, that when the Constitution falls we will lose our freedom as Americans! The message to Christians is to enter into repentance! When we humble ourselves before God, He will hear our cry, but it must be on a national scale. I cannot say how it is to be done. Recently, when Pastor Phil was in my church, the presence of God showed up. In God's presence the desire and knowledge of sin is revealed. Pursuing God is a national "must do." In His presence all kinds of wonderful things happen.

There is more in the Christian experience than the American Church has been experiencing. It is diluted and missing the power of the Holy Spirit that changes lives. The tangible spiritual life of God needs to be manifested in our churches. It needs to flow across America. I have told you this analogy before, but let me say it again. The spiritual life of God is likened to a bouquet of fresh-cut flowers. Dried-up spiritual life looks like a bouquet of silk flowers; they look good but they have no life in them. We have the silk flower version of Christianity.

Now don't get all offended. I heard a story once about a man who threw a rock into a pack of dogs. The dog that yelped was the one who got hit by the rock. I am not challenging churches already flowing in the new move of God. I am determined to reveal a big God we serve and the spiritual life we need. When we have the spiritual life of God flowing, He shows us His holiness and our sinfulness. It brings gratitude for the blessings that He has given to us. America is the best country in the world. It is a blessing from God. But as we become unholy and forsake God, the liberty and freedom we have known all our lives becomes at stake.

In My Dreams

Put yourself in my dreams! Think of how it would feel to lose your freedom and be torn from your family. This is the message Amos gave Israel. This is the same message I am sharing with you. As far as I am concerned, I have already tasted captivity and it motivates me to plead with God to intervene on our behalf. I hope it motivates you to seek God and live!

Will we do what it takes to humble ourselves before God?
Will we be willing to turn from our sins
and the comfort prosperity has given us?
Will we go out of our way to seek those places where
the presence of God appears?
Will we be renewed as a child of God?
For your sake—
For my sake—
For everyone's sake—
GET OFF THE FENCE!

Epilogue

Do you feel it? Do you feel the stirring of the Holy Spirit within your heart right now? Is it the beginning of repentance? Praise God! Enter into a time with the Lord, shedding your burdens and giving them to Him.

I want to make a suggestion. Go to your computer and bring up www.youtube.com. In the search window type in "Kutless": Take me in (to the holy of holies), and open a second window and do the same except do a search for "Jason Upton Glory Come Down Worship." These are two of my favorite songs when I am seeking the glory of God. You can put on your favorite worship music and turn your heart His way. There is no better time than right now to seek the Lord and humble yourself before Him. The most important thing you can do is enter the holy of holies. Spend as much time as you can in His presence.

You have been on a journey with me. I hope that it has stretched you to desire more in your relationship with God. There is a very serious message for us Americans.

This is what the Lord said to Israel: "Seek me and live" (Amos 5:4).

We need to seek God for His presence in our churches. We must be willing for God to show us our own sins. We must seek repentance personally and corporately in the Church. We need the spiritual life only God can send to flood the land. Christians know that we do have an enemy. We wrestle against demons, principalities, and the powers of darkness. They affect the heavenly flow we long for. We want it to be realized in our hearts. In Christ Jesus, the victory is ours.

Let me ask you this. Have you ever asked God to show you what is coming down the road ahead in your life? We are looking down the road, and I see the state of Texas being flooded with the inheritance of God. This results in the salvation of mankind. I see it spreading beyond the great state of Texas to the surrounding states. One-quarter of the United States, or sixty million people, are involved. We are quickly coming to a fork in the road of our spiritual and physical destiny.

Churches scattered across the region are defined in my vision. Special attention is given to those with unique pastors who have hearts like little children before the Lord. They will do great things. As more people are born again and gather into the Kingdom of God, the combined cry will be heard by Father God.

I look down the road at our future. Repentance is necessary or we will lose our freedom in America. We must repent and allow God to renew our spirits and hearts. Do we have too many fence-sitting Christians in our day? These are Christians who have one foot in the world and the other foot in the Kingdom of God.

My brother-in-law's testimony challenged us to get off the fence. Time is too short. There is no time for procrastinating and not taking action to seek God. We are eternal beings. Compare our short life on earth with the length of eternity. It is in this short period of time we can work for Jesus. Once our life is over, the opportunity to work for Him is gone. Don't miss the chance to contribute to His work while you still can. Remember the parable of the ten virgins? Five of the virgins waited for the bridegroom and brought extra oil for their lamps. We would say in our day: "They had a plan B." That extra oil represents the Holy Spirit, a close relationship that comes with spending time with Him. Examine your life right now and ask yourself, *Do I have the extra oil of the Holy Spirit in my life?* If you answer the question by saying no, now is the time to seek the Lord.

I am not a person to say you must or you should. It is the cry of my heart to motivate you into action. I have spent many hours praying for you, your families, and mine. I have seen the horrors of captivity in the dreams. The horror is due to the fall of the Constitution. Take to heart the prayers that I have written and apply the necessary ones to your lives. Ask God for the help to do just that. Look for a church that is seeking the presence of God. Or better yet, encourage your pastor to open the door to heaven and seek God and His presence for your congregation.

As Amos challenged the Israelites, their hearts were struck by his words. They had a choice to make. Christians here in America have a choice to make, as well. I hope my words have challenged you to examine your spiritual position. The question becomes, "Do we love our sins and lose our freedom? Or do we turn toward God and keep our freedom, receiving the increased blessing from God?"

This book is focused on what God has been sharing with me and my desire to share it with you. God is using other children to tell of the difficulties lying ahead of us as Americans. Hearing the messages from credible prophetic people coincides with the things I have shared with you. I say, let's find our way into the presence of God and receive His passion and glory. Let's start the fire burning in of our hearts all across our land.

I am speaking directly to you now. God loves you! He desires an intimate relationship with you today. He is hoping for you to enter into communion with Him. The Lord desires for you to have a more intimate relationship with Him. There is so much more for you to experience with Him. God's eyes are scanning the world to see who is coming to Him. Passionately He will run toward you with the embrace of a loving Father. It's time for you to put your sins aside. Please ask for the forgiveness of your sins and turn from them. Come into the cleansing of the blood of Jesus Christ.

Dear Father,

I lift up to You the person reading this prayer right now. I ask, Lord, that You would allow them to come into Your Presence and into Your weighted glory. Empty them of all the pain and trauma hiding in their hearts. Take all the effects of sin and wash it away. Release, Lord, the fullness of Your love into their hearts and fill them with Your living water. Wrap them in Your loving arms and whisper "I love you" in their ear. Forgive them, Father, of their sins. Forgive them of their iniquities and transgression and rebellion toward You, and cleanse them as only You can do. In Jesus' name we pray. Amen.

Epilogue

Note to pastors:

With dreams and visions, I like to come to a place of knowing that I understand them beyond a shadow of a doubt. I came to this position when the Lord recently showed me a Scripture:

"I am to be the only inheritance the priests have. You are to give them no possession in Israel; I will be their possession" (Ezekiel 44:28).

In three recent revival meetings with Pastor Phil, I have seen the presence of God arrive. He visited the church with His presence, and then I understood the inheritance. He is the inheritance!

May God bless you.

Endnotes

Chapter 1
1 R. Horchow, *The Art of Friendship*, New York, NY, 2005.

Chapter 3
1 N.P. Grubb, *Rees Howells Intercessor*, Philadelphia, PA: Christian Literature Crusade, 1952.

Chapter 5
1 Shirley Toulson, *The Celtic Year*, Thorsons, 1996.

Chapter 6
1 Todd Burpo and Lynn Vincent, *Heaven Is for Real*, Nashville: Thomas Nelson, 2010.
2 Kramarik, Akiane: *Her Life, Her Art, Her Poetry*, Nashville: W Publishing Group, 2006.
3 Don Piper, *90 Minutes in Heaven*, Grand Rapids, MI: Revell, 2004.
4 Word to the World Ministries, Website at www.w2wmin.org.
5 John Mark Pool, Path of a Prophet, Shippensburg, PA: Destiny Image, 2007.

Chapter 17
1 John Paul Jackson, Needless Causalities of War, Fort Worth, TX, 1999.

Chapter 18
1 Jim Goll, *The Seer*, Shippensburg, PA: Destiny Image Publishers, 2005.

Chapter 19
1 *Matthew Henry's Commentary*, Internet website, biblestudytools.com (Concise commentary on the Whole Bible) or ccel.org, Christian classics Ethereal Library, 1706.

Chapter 22

1 M.W. Etter, *Signs and Wonders,* New Kinsington, Whitaker House, 1997

2 Anderson, *The Bondage Breaker,* 2006.

Chapter 23

1 Price, *The Prophets' Dictionary,* 2006.

2 Milligan, *Understanding the Dreams You Dream*, 1997.

Chapter 24

1 *Matthew Henry's Commentary.*

About the Author

Tom Donnan was pronounced clinically dead of a heart attack in February 2006. But God wasn't done with him. He brought Tom back to the land of the living with a burden to see revival come to America. He frequently travels and ministers with Pastor Phillip Corbett. He's married to Mary, his wife of 13 years, and has three grandchildren.

Email: HealingTheNation1776@gmail.com

Facebook: Healing The Nation Ministries